D1383888

The Voice of the Natives
THE CANADIAN NORTH
and ALASKA

August 1, 2001

"THE VOICES OF THE NATIVES …THE Canadian North and Alaska" by Hans Blohm is a true representation of the Northern People.

While working with Nunavut Tunngavik Inc., an Inuit Land Claims Organization that is administering Nunavut Land Claims on behalf of some 24,000 Inuit beneficiaries in Nunavut, Hans has recorded the history of Inuit in Nunavut. Hans has traveled extensively throughout the Arctic Regions of Canada and Alaska.

He has documented the hopes and visions of our Elders. He documented the Youth of Nunavut, drumming for joy, promoting the happiness and joys of our people. Through his camera lens, Hans has helped to protect, preserve and promote Inuit culture. That is good for all people – Northerners and Southerners alike

This beautiful book is about passing the wisdom and knowledge of the Elders to the youth, our future. "THE VOICE OF THE NATIVES…" will allow you, the reader, to see for yourself, the faces of the North.

This Pictorial book and essays, is what we Northerners are all about.

Hans is a true "Ambassador". He is our voice in southern Canada and the world. He has also become a good friend of us Northerners – we trust him.

Peter Irniq,
Commissioner of Nunavut

The Voice of the Natives
THE CANADIAN NORTH
and ALASKA

Penumbra Press

Für Rudi,
mit recht herzlichem Dank
für all den guten Rat –
und das gute Ohr – und die guten Augen!
In alter Freundschaft!
Hans   Nov. 2001

Photography by Hans-Ludwig Blohm

PUBLISHER'S FOREWORD

Colour Photography Copyright © Hans-L Blohm, 2001
Text Copyright © the Authors and Penumbra Press, 2001
Archival Photos Copyright © the Proprietors, 2001

All rights reserved. No part of this book covered by the copyrights hereon may be reproduced or used in any form or by any means — graphic, electronic, or mechanical — without the prior written permission of the publisher. Any request for photocopying, recording, taping, or storage or retrieval systems of any part of this book shall be directed in writing to CanCopy, Toronto.

Cover concept: Sean Horton
Interior design: Collin R. Young, Point 5 Inc., Ottawa
Copy editing: Douglas Campbell and Evangeline Campbell
Printed in Canada by M.O.M. Printing
Published by Penumbra Press

NATIONAL LIBRARY OF CANADA CATALOGUING
IN PUBLICATION DATA

Blohm, Hans
The voice of the natives : the Canadian north and Alaska

Includes photos and text by Hans Blohm with essays by northern Native people
ISBN 1-894131-13-4

1. Native peoples—Canada Northern—Pictorial works.
2. Indigenous peoples—Alaska—Pictorial works. 3. Native peoples—Canada, Northern. 4. Indigenous peoples—Alaska. I Title.
E77.B59 2001a 971.9'00497'0222 C2001-902284-0

Many years ago I had the pleasure of collaborating with Hans Blohm on a project that would become one of Penumbra Press's first books, a facsimile edition of a sketchbook by J.E.H. MacDonald in the collection at the National Gallery of Canada. His task was to photograph every page of the sketchbook under studio conditions for the purpose of reproducing them in book form. As he arranged his equipment and went on with the assignment, I was enormously impressed by his dedication to both the craft and the profession of photography. The end result became a magnificent testament both to his work and to MacDonald's.

At that time I was unaware of his other love: the love of the north, especially the sub-polar north that was well beyond my familiar geography of northern Ontario. In the years since the MacDonald book, Hans has travelled thousands of miles in all parts of the north, sometimes by land and sometimes by air, but always with the thrill and enthusiasm of an explorer who is making new discoveries. It is especially the people of the north that draw him back year after year, sometimes for months.

The Voice of the Natives is a partial record of those trips, pictorially and textually. With cameras always at his side or slung over his shoulder, Hans can be counted on for breath-taking photos of the people and the land. Half of this book comprises a photographic interpretation of those trips. The other half contains visceral accounts of his travels as well as poignant essays and contributions he solicited from Inuit and northern authors whose own sensibility and first hand experience helped to show him the way and further shape his understanding.

In addition, *The Voice of the Natives* includes a "photographic essay" made up of archival black and white photographs from various public collections. The purpose of including these photos is to offer a counterpoint for readers — to balance the two very different worlds occupied by the people. To some readers the decision to place the archival photographs in an apparently random fashion throughout the text portion of the book may seem quixotic. Although the photos neither illustrate nor explain the texts — they have no immediate or direct inter-connection — they do provide a visual narrative that permits one to drop back in time while reading about present circumstances and events. The effect of this juxtaposition is to make us more conscious of life before the Qallunaat came and perhaps, through a kind of role reversal, to evaluate our own "complicity" in the inevitable consequences.

Furthermore, to accentuate the contemporary nature of the black and white photos as well as the method in which they were catalogued and described by their collectors, we have elected to retain the captions printed on the labels attached to the back of the photos. In this way, we can appreciate how the "voices" of the north were heard by these early chroniclers.

The Voice of the Natives is therefore a challenge on many levels. It is a book that bridges many centuries of promise: it enlightens and instructs as well as fascinates and enthralls.

The publisher wishes to thank the many contributors and supporters of *The Voice of the Natives*, among them Nunavut Tungavik Incorporated; Makivik Corporation; The Inuvialuit Regional Corporation; Lowepro; First Air; Inuit Tapirisat of Canada; The Canada Council for the Arts; and the Ontario Arts Council.

Thanks also to Douglas and Evangeline Campbell for copy editing the manuscripts; to Sean Horton for graphics; to Collin Young at Point 5 Inc. for design; to John Colyer at M.O.M. Printing for pre-press guidance; to Hans Blohm for conceiving such a wonderful project; and to the authors whose essays and writings convey a natural but necessary insight.

— John Flood

ACKNOWLEDGEMENTS

As the gestation period for this book was an exceedingly long one, so too is the list for "thank you's."

First and foremost I am grateful to the Northerners who allowed me a glimpse into their soul through their writings and their openness toward me, an outsider. I am humbled and elated in their presence. Many an encounter became seared into my mind.

Travelling on a "shoe string," as I had to do over the years, made even the smallest help in the form of shelter, food, logistics, and advice, very meaningful to me. Many photographs came about during work on other projects, such as assignments for *Makivik News* magazine, under the editorship of Stephen Hendrie; as well as assignments for *Canadian Geographic* magazine; Stelco and Dofasco steel companies of Hamilton, Ontario, with Spencer Dunmore and Robert James respectively; and Indian and Northern Affairs, and Public Works Canada.

The vast areas of the North made the use of aircraft mandatory: Canada's "First Air," under President Bob Davis, and "Air Inuit," both owned by the Inuit of Makivik Corp. of Nunavik; "Frontier Flying Service Inc.," owned and operated by the Hajdukovich family of Fairbanks, Alaska; particularly Lynn Hajdukovich, whose charm and enthusiasm coupled with superb rapport with the people of Alaska opened many doors for me.

My good friend Claus-M Naske and his wife Dinah also of Fairbanks, Alaska, with their "Open House" toward me. (And their steady supply of smoked salmon, by the pound.)

Helmut Schoener, the "flying dentist" and aircraft builder pilot out of Dawson City, Yukon. A friend of very longstanding and great understanding of this long term project.

My "Eagle" friends, the Piepgras, Judi and Ken, out of Soldotna, Alaska.

Margaret Thompson of the Gwitch'in Nation in Fort McPherson/NWT.

The two Pfeiffers — Reg the pilot and "uncle" Harold the sculptor of northern people, both dead now, crisscrossing with me the Canadian and Alaska's north in their floatplane for over three weeks — gave me a distinctly different perspective of the lay of the land.

And Yes, the sailing vessel *Manakoora* under the guidance of Camille Choquette and crew, exploring, for weeks, every uninhabited fiord on the coast of Labrador, north of Nain. Navigating under all weather conditions, between icebergs and island passages. Unforgettable.

On the three MacKenzie River Ice road trips by my own car to Tuktoyaktuk: Hildegard and Walter Willkomm of the MacKenzie Hotel, as generous hosts in Inuvik on one end and Emma and Fritz Feichtinger in "Tuk" on the other, in the dead of winter.

At he very beginning of my work on this undertaking, there was Martine Bresson, a superb lady and amateur photographer. Generous soul that she is, she made it financially possible for me to present an early dummy of this book at the International Book fair in Frankfurt, Germany to various international publishers.

For the use of archival photography I am grateful to the National Archives of Canada, Ottawa; the RCMP Museum, Regina; Yukon Archives, Whitehorse; and the Historic Photograph Collection in the Archives and Polar Regions Department, University of Alaska in Fairbanks.

I THANK YOU ALL for your generosity and spirit.

— Hans-Ludwig Blohm

DEDICATION

I dedicate this book to the people of the North, whom I have learned to love and respect.

— Hans-Ludwig Blohm

CONTENTS

"ARE YOU FINISHED, WHITE MAN? I AM SPEAKING."

Hans-Ludwig Blohm

These words startled and shamed me. They were spoken by an elderly Indian woman who was conducting a guided tour at the Ksan Indian village near Hazelton in British Columbia. My 17-year-old daughter Heike and I were on our way back from the Yukon and Alaska in August 1977.

We had travelled in our trusted Volvo station wagon from Ottawa diagonally across this vast continent, up the Alaska and Klondike Highways, still unpaved and rough, and, as far as one could, up the unfinished Dempster Highway, then back to Dawson City. From there we crossed the Yukon River and followed the spectacular "Top up the World" road to Alaska. The mighty Denali (Mount McKinley) took us in its grip when we tented near Wonder Lake. Then it was back home to Ottawa. Our route had followed the Cassiar–Stewart Highway, with a stopover at Hyder, the southernmost point on the Alaska panhandle. Population: 7.

By the time we had reached Ksan village we were seasoned travellers; we had encountered many native people and had walked or driven through many communities. At the native-run campground next to Ksan, where we had pitched our small tent beside the Kispiox River for the night, we learned that next morning we could take a guided tour of the newly-erected traditional native longhouses.

These three beautiful longhouses had various designations. The oldest one was called B.C. — not for "Before Christ," but for "Before Contact" — before contact with the intruding white people. I found it remarkable that such an unusual meaning for the initials B.C. would be given such prominence.

When I entered B.C. I took note of the very low light level. The main light came through a central opening in the ceiling, which let the smoke from the cooking and heating escape. The Leica camera and the film I was using could not cope with the lack of light. So I went to my car and picked up the Leica M5 rangefinder camera with the very fast f1.0 Noctilux lens and faster colour slide film.

When I returned, my eyes had to adjust to the dim interior, so I remained at the entrance. Then I lifted the Leica and looked toward the small group of perhaps eight people listening to the guide. Suddenly she stopped her explanation, looked straight at me, and quietly spoke, with dignity, but with emphasis: "Are you finished, white man? I am speaking."

I had trespassed. I had not asked permission to be in her home! I had definitely been put on the spot. I felt like turning into a mouse and disappearing into a hole somewhere.

After the elder completed her tour I apologized. She graciously accepted my apology. We had a lengthy conversation, which neither my daughter Heike nor I will ever forget. She spoke about her people — about their traditions, about their struggle to survive as a distinct group. Particularly, she spoke to us about their fight to retain their language, which she recognized as most important for their cultural survival.

With a gleam in her brown eyes she reported that after a fight lasting more than thirty years, they had been given permission — "permission" from the British Columbia provincial government — to teach their age-old mother tongue to their children. How can the "authorities" give permission to follow the laws of nature? The language restriction was an imposition of the first order. I see it simply as a power play.

She could begin to talk again to her grandchildren in her own language. There was hope now that her culture would survive. However, she could not talk to her own children. They did not know that language. They were the children who had been stolen from their homes and put into uniforms in missionary schools. There they learned about a foreign God, a personalized God who was alien to all their traditions and experiences — one who punished and rewarded, one who forbade your mother tongue, one who made you a stranger to your parents and your elders; one who tried to cut you off from your roots; one who ignored what you know and replaced it with strange teachings. One who insisted that you obey only him; one who instilled fear and anxiety. One who declared that your non-Christian ancestors were evil savages, even brute beasts.

After this long chat, we parted as friends.

This encounter in the B.C. longhouse lingered in our thoughts. Time and again our memory was drawn back to the face and the voice and the gleam in the eyes of the village elder. On the long drive from Ksan, British Columbia to Ottawa, Ontario, there was plenty of time for thought. This experience was the beginning of my long initiation in the ways of the North.

* * *

(Eskimo) at little Whale River (P.Q.) ca. 1865.

PHOTOGRAPH BY GEORGE SIMPSON MCTAVISH — COURTESY OF THE NATIONAL ARCHIVES OF CANADA, C3408.

home to Ottawa. The seeds were planted then for a book on this beautiful part of the North American continent. The idea has lingered in my mind for some time.

PHOTOGRAPHING THE NORTH

Several more trips ensued over the years. One, devoted to photography, took place during the record cold winter of 1978-79. We travelled some 20,000 to 25,000 kilometres in my trusted Volvo station wagon. My colleague Juergen Kittel, a Leica technician, and I had planned this trip very carefully. We assembled a load of survival gear. Our Leica cameras had been prepared with a special low-temperature lubricant that the Leitz company had flown in from Germany. They were ready to withstand the very low temperatures we might encounter. And encounter them we did. The drive through the Canadian prairies gave us a taste of things to come.

Despite the -30°C temperature I had a swim in Liard Hot Springs, halfway up the Alaska Highway. After the frigid undressing it was wonderfully hot and soothing. A wreath of ice soon adorned my hair. The flow from this natural spring-fed hot-water pool steamed and rose to form hoarfrost on all the trees around the pool, creating exquisite shapes of glistening white and silver against a deep blue sky. The natives of the region have used the hot spring as a source of inspiration for body and soul since time immemorial.

The famous Dempster Highway was completed

My encounter with the thought-provoking Ksan guide took place some time after I had met former Gwich'in Indian Chief, Joe Henry, and his wife Annie. They lived alone, and still do, on the Dempster Highway. Joe Henry, so we have been told, living off the land in the way of his ancestors, had shot a moose out of season — out of white man's season — to restock his larder. Caught (not that he tried to hide) and charged, he had to appear in court. The charges were subsequently dropped. Somebody in the white justice system had second thoughts. Henry just laughed at the white man's folly. He went home and enjoyed his moose meat. Had the white lawmakers consulted any natives, I wondered, before imposing their alien law in the North?

In the fall of 1976 I took my first drive up the famous Alaska Highway, through that magnificent part of British Columbia, the Yukon, and Alaska. The highlight of that trip was an Alaska Ferry ride down and up the Panhandle — down to Ketchikan from Haines, and back to Haines. By mid-October there was deep snow and mud along the upper reaches of the road to Haines Junction at the Alaska Highway, where we met many natives and saw many remnants of their culture. We also saw and felt the influence of the earlier Russian colonization of that part of Alaska.

All these things came back to me during our trip

in the fall of 1978, in time for our arrival in the middle of January 1979. Juergen and I were headed for the Eagle River crossing, where the Canadian Army Corps of Engineers had built, as a special winter exercise, the largest steel bridge of its kind erected that far north. They wanted to keep this alleged all-weather road open during this, its first winter. We had to obtain special permission from the Highway section of Indian and Northern Affairs in Ottawa to use it and then report to the Yukon Government Highway Department in Whitehorse. Once our Volvo was inspected and passed, together with our survival gear and food supply, we headed up the Klondike Highway from Whitehorse to Dawson City.

In the middle of January, daylight hours become fewer the farther north one goes. Twilight hours transform the landscape in many different ways. Colour changes are subtle. If the sun is out, the white snow takes on hues of purple and pink. To newcomers, it seems like a fairy tale. The temperature kept dropping. At several locations gasoline pumps, vital to keep our engine running and to keep us warm, were frozen. It was even hard to open the door of the Volvo, despite the special graphite lubricant on the hinges.

Traffic on the road eventually ceased. The entire southern Yukon was in a deep freeze. We got to the Dempster cut-off, the junction of the Klondike and Dempster Highways, some 50 kilometres outside of Dawson City. The large Esso station, with its workshop and motel, run for many years by the McGillivry family, provided a warm shelter. There we met the snow-removal crews who were working around the clock to clear the Dempster through to the Northwest Territories border, where the NWT crews would take over. They kept three big D8 Caterpillar diesel-powered shovels working on the

fine powdered snow blown onto the road in the North Fork Pass area. With our chains for the tires ready, we set off, following the crew.

The slow drive through the forested lower sections of the Dempster, and the gradual climb into the Ogilvie Mountains, snow-covered and gleaming, was immensely beautiful. The wind covered everything with blowing powdered snow and ice fog. Our Leicas did not once let us down, although the shutters sounded strange in the cold, and we had to advance the brittle film ever so slowly in order not to break it.

Up in the North Fork Pass area we realized what a tough task the snow-removal crews faced. Small bridges over rivers and creeks had to be cleared by hand. The wind howled down the barely visible slopes and buffeted the car. For three days we remained close to the "battlefront." Sometimes during breaks we warmed our feet on the hot Cats. Altogether, only eight miles were cleared during our time with the crews. Then all traffic was officially stopped, even on the Klondike Highway. We obtained some rather good photographs, but our hopes to see the Eagle Plains Bridge could not be realized.

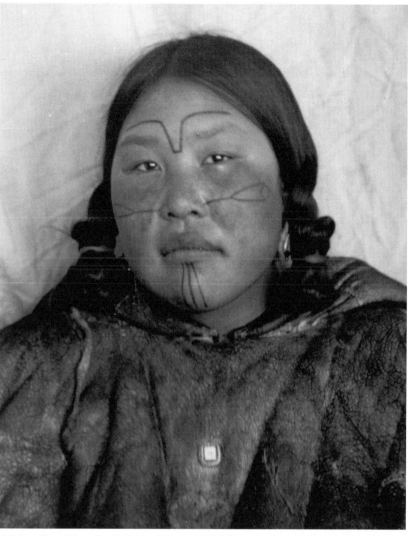

A.P. Low Expedition. Southampton Island (N.W.T.) Woman tattooed (like North Baffin Land Natives).

PHOTOGRAPH BY A.P. LOW — COURTESY OF THE NATIONAL ARCHIVES OF CANADA, PA50920 — GEOLOGICAL SURVEY OF CANADA COLLECTION.

We decided to charter a small plane out of Dawson, but no pilot wanted to risk a flight up the Dempster in such hazardous weather. Eventually our good friend Julie Frisch in Dawson City per-

Interior of large igloo near Chesterfield Inlet.

PHOTOGRAPH BY NFB — COURTESY OF THE NATIONAL ARCHIVES OF CANADA, PA117138.

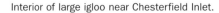

suaded the outfitter Stan Reynolds to fly his ski-equipped Cessna from his small private airstrip. If the sun came through, the best time to fly would be around noon.

Full of excitement, we left early to get on our way past the Cat crews in North Fork Pass. We had no radio or other contact with Stan Reynolds, but the weather seemed to have cleared up. However, as we drove south the weather suddenly changed to an almost total whiteout. We had to abandon our trip and return to the North Fork Pass. After we got to the motel very late we learned that perfect flying weather had prevailed at Stan's all day long.

We were shattered. We had missed an opportunity.

It disturbed me no end not to have achieved our goal. In Whitehorse once again, we kept searching for a plane to fly us up to the Eagle River. We finally found one at a flying school. They had a 172 Cessna that had just been re-assembled after an overhaul. They were licensed for sight-seeing only. And that was all we wanted. A young Danish pilot was eager to go.

It was a grand flight over the roadway, the settlements of Carmacks, Pelly Crossing, and Stewart Crossing, and the mighty frozen Yukon River with its myriad of meanders.

At the small Dawson City airport we filed our flight plan and refuelled. We were advised to refuel on the return leg at Mayo, which, unlike Dawson City, had lights on its strip. The temperatures

remained low. A damned good pilot, I thought — he reacted precisely to get us in position for aerial photography. We had to cover about 550 kilometres as the crow flies before touching ground again at Mayo.

It was thrilling to fly farther and farther north, sometimes very close to the mountainsides and ridges. I was oblivious to time's passing, though I did notice that the Kodachrome film got progressively slower in the fading light of the fast-approaching sub-Arctic night. The sun dipped below the horizon, and we were still heading north. We flew over the newly erected Eagle Plains Hotel, with its small emergency airstrip; its lights were blinking, begging us to spend the night there safe and warm.

We had flown for many hours in a cramped little plane. It was tempting to go down, but I decided to carry on. With the last glimmer of light, we recorded many animal tracks along the shores of the Eagle River and underneath the Eagle River Bridge. Darkness was falling fast when we turned south. I had a funny feeling in the pit of my stomach, as our little plane flew on, unequipped with instruments for night flying. A slim red line still marked the western horizon.

We had sufficient fuel to return to Mayo. Our pilot tried to radio the Mayo airport — no reply. We were already approaching Mayo. W tried again — still no response. The pilot ignored my advice to head for Dawson City. I checked

Eskimo women, Aklavik, N.W.T., ca. 1926.

PHOTOGRAPH BY J.F. MORAN — COURTESY OF THE NATIONAL ARCHIVES OF CANADA,
PA102513 — INDIAN AND NORTHERN AFFAIRS COLLECTION.

the fuel gauge and insisted he change direction. The three of us began to feel a little uneasy, in mid-January, in that pitch-dark Arctic night, in a puny one-engined plane on wheels, with diminishing fuel and no radio contact.

Slowing to conserve fuel, searching the terrain with our headlights, we made our way beside mountain walls. The pilot searched for an emergency landing strip while trying to contact Dawson. After some nerve-wracking navigation we picked out a faint light and used it as a guide. We corkscrewed up to a higher altitude, where we were able finally to talk to Dawson. Although their advice was to fly on, we told them we had no choice, we were out of fuel. We were coming down.

The controller said he would set out firepots to guide us in, and soon, circling over the airstrip and above the surrounding mountains, we saw a pickup truck depositing the pots. The fuel gauge registered zero when we bumped to the ground and rolled out. The truck rushed up to us, and so did the radio operator, who had by now left his post. The five of us started laughing our heads off at the end of that tiny runway, the small fire-pots flickering around us in the -42°C Arctic night.

The truck driver got us into Dawson, where we spent the night. The next morning the air was full of ice-fog — not flying weather. Around noon we were cleared for takeoff. We set out to return to Whitehorse, but visibility was poor, so we stayed low over the Klondike Highway. Clouds appeared on the horizon, and against all the rules the pilot

corkscrewed us up to a wonderful world of sunshine and blue sky. Mountaintops broke through the clouds. In the distance gleamed the Alaska and Wrangell Ranges, while below us were smaller mountaintops with snow-laden trees. It was a photographer's paradise. But the plane began to ice up, rapidly. As the ice built up on the wings and the windows, we realized we were in great danger. We had to land immediately. Miraculously, we were able to find an emergency airstrip.

We landed, barely in control, on the famous "Cinnamon Bun" strip, really just a widened section of the road next to a service station. It took hard work and ingenuity to remove the ice from the plane. After some hot soup, a cinnamon bun, and some coffee to restore the flyers, we returned to Whitehorse, relieved and exhausted. Our young

pilot almost broke down as he confessed that he'd never been to Dawson or flown above the clouds. At 23 he would have years ahead of him to make use of the day's experience, and, more important, to gain lots more, which, we had learned, is what you want most in someone flying you around the north.

PLANES, PIPELINES, AND EAGLES

Although all vehicles except for supply trucks were forbidden to go into Prudhoe Bay, the large oil project in the Beaufort Sea, we drove up the North Haul Road (now called the Dalton Highway) as far as we could. At the Yukon River crossing a guard stopped us and turned us back. On a hill overlooking the Yukon River Bridge we talked to another

Leaf River Eskimos with flags (N.W.T.), ca. 1931.

PHOTOGRAPH BY CORP. MCINNIS — COURTESY OF THE NATIONAL ARCHIVES OF CANADA,
PA102550 — INDIAN AND NORTHERN AFFAIRS COLLECTION.

guard at a pipeline station. His ruling: no entry and no photos. We could see the pipeline down in the valley snaking its way toward a bridge that carries it across a deep canyon.

We headed back toward Fairbanks. There we stayed for two days before heading south on the Alaska Highway toward Haines Junction in the Yukon and there turning west toward the Alaska "panhandle" and the town of Haines. At the airstrip we chartered another plane, a low wing Piper, to take us into Glacier Bay, across the Alsek and Chilkat Ranges. Alaska has by far the largest number of small aircraft and pilots in the world, and, sadly, the highest rate of accidents and fatalities. The huge landmass, the diverse climatic and geographic zones, the lack of roads, and the comparatively sparse population, all contribute to the alarming aircraft statistics.

One of the sights I was determined to see was the "eagle council," a congregation of bald-headed eagles in the northern rain forest cottonwood stands in the Chilkat River area. The banks of the river are strewn with tens of thousands of salmon, dead after having completed their spawning cycle. Between 1,500 and 2,500 birds are attracted there to feed. They begin to gather in late October and stay till spring, when they fly back to their summer ranges in southwestern Alaska, the Yukon, and northern British Columbia.

It was almost warm, the sky was blue, and there was little wind. It was not the most convenient plane to use for photography, but the pilot and I were able to work out ways to accomplish some good work.

We swept over the tall cottonwoods along the Chilkat River and saw the eagles sitting in them like so many starlings gathering for migration. It is an unbelievable sight. We stayed high and used the 90 and 180 mm lenses so as not to disturb the birds.

Then we were off over the mountains into Glacier Bay. The vast mountain ranges and glaciers, the Pacific in the distance, and the gleaming snow inspired us to take roll after roll of film.

Our allotted time was running out. We had to return to Haines, and then back to the Yukon. It was risky to start so very late in the afternoon to return by the Haines Road. Anticipating the steep inclines and the packed snow, we decided to put snow-chains on the rear tires. Even so we barely made it through the Chilkat Pass (1065 metres). I took a last look. The eerie light of a full moon over the St. Elias range was a beautiful sight with which to end the day's experience.

We did get back safe and sound, and left early next morning for the long drive back through the Yukon, British Columbia, Alberta, Saskatchewan, Manitoba, and Ontario, once again following the northern route of the Trans-Canada Highway around the Great Lakes.

FIRST CONTACT

I recalled my first contact with the people of the Arctic. It occurred in October 1978, before a big winter trip to the Yukon and Alaska. I had a chance to take some photographs at a meeting of settlement elders at Pond Inlet, at the northern tip of Baffin Island in the eastern Canadian Arctic. Most of the elders sitting around a huge ring of tables in the school auditorium were unilingual Inuktitut-speakers.

Arctic Explorations – Young men, Rigolet (Labrador) Sept. 28th 1924.

PHOTOGRAPH BY L.T. BURWASH – COURTESY OF THE NATIONAL ARCHIVES OF CANADA,
PA99251 – INDIAN AND NORTHERN AFFAIRS COLLECTION.

The organizers of this meeting, the Canadian Department of Indian and Northern Affairs, had flown in equipment for instantaneous translation from Montreal — necessary because the proceedings were conducted in English. In front of each delegate was a microphone. The translators' booth was off in a corner. I clearly recall how the faces of the Inuit lit up when one of the white people, Nigel Wilford, spoke in their native tongue (he had spent over a decade in the Arctic). A different, more humane tone was immediately noticeable. When English once again dominated the proceedings the discussion reverted to a subdued, sombre tone.

While in Pond Inlet I visited the Arctic Research Establishment: "Sea-Ice and Oceanography," which was operated by Hermann Steltner, a German-born Canadian engineer. I photographed Inuit women and men using scientific instruments in a laboratory. A young mother, with her baby on her back in the traditional way, was bent over a calculator. At first she startled me, but to her it was quite natural. One of Steltner's jobs was to level-in the foundation pilings of a new Hudson's Bay store to be build in Pond. The levelling instrument was operated by an Inuk as if it was the most natural thing for him to do.

Hermann Steltner told me of the laboratory's beginnings years earlier. He had moved north with the idea of measuring the flow and salinity of sea-ice. This was looked upon by the local white community as slightly ludicrous. As his staff he used Inuit exclusively, against the advice of the white

establishment. They were sure that natives could not perform scientific tasks. Steltner laughed, and the natives proved him right. Their natural curiosity and power of observation proved to be great assets. Steltner taught them the rest. His Institute became renowned throughout the Northern hemisphere.

My flight from Arctic Bay and Nanisivik to Pond Inlet gave me tremendous views of the country and the sea below. We flew one of the famous Canadian Twin Otters, operated by Bradley Air Services from Ottawa. I took the co-pilot's seat for a while in order to shoot some pictures through a small flap in the side window. It was October, with plenty of new snow on the ground and on the mountains. Sea-ice was forming on Eclipse Sound between Bylot and Baffin Islands. A Canadian Coastguard icebreaker was making its way through the ice floes. I learned later that I had caught the ice about 24 hours before it froze solid.

It is a big country up there — powerful and almost intimidating; harsh, yet immensely beautiful and fragile. I gained a tremendous respect for the people who managed to survive there, who thrived and evolved. Who showed inner strength and resourcefulness. Who are cheerful once the essentials to sustain life have been achieved. Where help is given and accepted naturally. They seem to be truly free.

What had the white man done to the natives by coming uninvited into their ancestral home territory? How do they really feel about our domineering presence? Were they ever asked?

I knew about treaties and reserves, about missionaries, about Hudson's Bay traders, about traders from the North-West Company, and, of course, about the police, the Mounties. I knew about the wars between the various white colonial armies to achieve dominance over the newly "discovered" lands. I also knew about the fighting between the various native groups and how the animosities among them had been exploited by the European newcomers to this continent.

But what had contact with the white people really done to the natives? Our diseases had decimated their populations. Our alcohol had rendered their minds and bodies less resistant to our ways. The mercantile thinking of the traders found easy victims in drunk natives. Baubles, alcohol, and guns changed hands, or, as the white conquerors liked to think, were "traded" for furs.

The enticement for the natives was great. More and more animals were killed for trade in furs, and killing became more efficient when native hunters were supplied with traps and firearms. The wildlife were decimated by the native trappers on the white man's behalf. The normal kill by the natives for food, clothing, and shelter would never have caused the depleted state of the wildlife we see today.

While traders were seeking furs, missionaries were seeking converts. The Jesuits were perhaps the most zealous, but other Christian denominations moved in as well. At one point Alaska was divided, one section for the Catholics, one section for the Anglicans, and so on. In strict European business style, it was divide and rule.

The God of all the missionaries demanded that the "savages" be converted to the only true religion. To serve Him no sacrifice was deemed to be too great. Everybody had to bow down. Before any conversion could be achieved, the existing beliefs, world views, and value systems had to be uprooted and destroyed. It was what the Christians had done to my own Germanic ancestors, centuries ago, with devastating and lasting negative effect.

All these things went through my mind as we drove across the country.

Many years later I obtained an essay from Armand Tagoona, from the central Arctic, the first Inuk to be ordained as a Christian priest. His essay startled me, coming from a native who had become an Anglican priest. However, he confirmed many of my own observations and conclusions. Armand Tagoona is dead now. He died about two weeks after I met him in Baker Lake in December 1991. His story sadly demonstrates once more how the white man played havoc with a conquered people.

What was and what is still wrong with us, with our attitude to life, with our conception of our place in the nature of things? Why have we lacked common decency toward our fellow man and thought ourselves to be better, with orders direct from the Christians' God to subdue everybody else? The powerful hierarchies of the churches have ruled, and still try to rule, with an iron fist. Unbelievers and deserters were once burned at the stake. Women did not have souls. The long-term effects of such doctrines continue to be devastating.

The faithful looked upon themselves as a chosen people, imbued with special privileges and a duty to convert others, by force if necessary, to the "only true faith."

INTRODUCTION TO JOHN AMAGOALIK

John Amagoalik is a remarkable Inuit leader who was instrumental in the drive for greater political independence and economic self-sufficiency for his people. I met him in Ottawa in February 1992.

Born in 1947 in a hunting camp near Inukjuak in northern Quebec, he was raised in Resolute Bay on Cornwallis Island, where his family was moved in 1953 as the result of the federal government's decision to relocate seventeen Inuit families, now often called "the High Arctic exiles." Amagoalik recalls that "the first two or three years in Resolute were extremely difficult for us. We grew up in Quebec on a diet of fish, game birds, caribou, and small mammals. But in Resolute, it was seal, walrus, and polar bear. It's very very different." After an early childhood spent largely in the tents and igloos of Inuit hunting camps, Amagoalik was sent, at the age of thirteen, to a boarding school in Churchill, Manitoba.

In 1962, the government flew him to Edmonton to be treated for tuberculosis. He stayed there for fourteen months. After he returned to the Arctic, Nigel Wilford, then assistant regional director of the Northwest Territories government, recruited him as an information officer. Amagoalik quickly established a reputation for his writing, both in English and in Inuit languages. In 1975 he joined the Inuit Tapirisat of Canada, and served as its president from 1981 to 1991. His role in the negotiations leading to the creation of Nunavut was such that he is now often referred to as the "father of Nunavut."

In "What Is This Land?" he writes about his feelings for his land. His words touched me profoundly. Reading them, I feel a deep kinship, as if he were speaking the thoughts of my ancestors. **HB**

WHAT IS THIS LAND?

John Amagoalik

The land is cold. The land is immense. It is a desert. It is unforgiving. It can be cruel. The land is also home. It sustains life. It breathes. It can bleed. It is part of our mother, the earth. It is beautiful. It nourishes our culture. We are part of it as it is part of us. We are one!

The Inuit of the world have a special spiritual relationship with the land. The European concept that land is for selling and buying was inconceivable to us. Also their idea that nature was something to be conquered is absurd. The Inuit have always understood that in order for the land to sustain us, we must treat it with respect. The land gives and takes.

Long before the great medieval wars in Europe, long before Christianity, long before the many dynasties of China, and thousands of generations before Columbus, the Arctic was home to the Inuit. The land shaped our mind and language, our culture, our legends, our philosophy and our view of life.

The Inuit law of survival called for co-operation, sharing and generosity. We regard other living things as integral parts of the whole and therefore must sustain their integrity. We understand that waste now means want later. We know that there must be a balance between take and return. Our environment has dictated these laws to us. They have sustained us for millenniums. They can still do so today.

The newcomers to our lands have finally begun to understand that we Inuit know a lot more than they thought we were capable of. They have started to come around to our way of thinking. They have started talking about "sustainable development, respect for the environment, conservation, ecosystems." Terms we have lived with and practiced for hundreds of decades.

They have begun to realize that they are wasteful, they have very dirty habits with their garbage, they expect too much material things out of life, they are too hostile and paranoid. They have too little trust for their fellow human beings, and are perhaps a little on the greedy side.

The world revolution in human rights is beginning to make it easier for us to live among them and for them to respect us and our homeland. Inuit have maintained a special kinship with animals of the land and creatures of the sea. We do not portray animals as cartoon characters but as sisters and brothers.

A.P. Low Expedition. Inside snowhouses (sic) Fullerton (N.W.T.).

PHOTOGRAPH BY A.P. LOW — COURTESY OF THE NATIONAL ARCHIVES OF CANADA, PA53566 —
GEOLOGICAL SURVEY OF CANADA COLLECTION.

Our legends, music and games reflect our preoccupation with the environment and the animals and spirits which surround us.

Our art expresses our mystical fascination with other living things. In our mind's eye, the wolf can turn into a bear or human being. We can fly to the moon. Our spirits can travel beyond our physical being. Good and bad spirits visit our lives. We name our children after species of animals and our ancestors. All these things demonstrate our intimate embrace with nature.

I have told many people over the years that it is important for Inuit political leaders to go out on the land at least once a year.

"Why is that important?" they ask. I tell them this: "When you are meeting with national and international leaders and others in positions of power and authority, sometimes you begin to feel big and important yourself. It is when you go back to the land that you realize just how small and insignificant you really are. The land's hugeness, its strength and beauty can overwhelm and humble you."

CONFLICT OF POWERS

Hans-Ludwig Blohm

Deep down I know that my ancestors — the Vikings and the Germanic tribes of Angles and Saxons — lived by mother nature's rules, as have all the peoples of the world. Our gradual alienation from these rules has made us a threat to the continuation of human life.

We have allowed power structures to take over: the world religions and their institutions, industrial-military complexes, international monetary interests, and the huge bureaucracies of government, even the democratic ones. Such organizations have evolved into systems that enslave us.

They have brought us religious dictatorship with its intolerance and demands for absolute obedience.

They have brought us nuclear science, with its frightening, life-threatening chain reactions. Instead of serving us, technology has taken on an insane life of its own, as witness the tinkering with human genetics.

We are bombarded with masses of information. Advertisements create desires for material things we do not need and cannot afford. Our resources are depleted, and our debts, both public and personal, are crippling. We see our individuality and independence drained away by faceless international corporations. We have all become slaves of systems and power-structures.

Where is the human dignity? Where is harmony of body and soul?

Where is tolerance for difference?

Where is the meaning of life? What is the meaning?

Compare what I see in our world to the harmonious life outlined in the Amagoalik essay.

Windy River, (N.W.T.) Taking the census and also checking on Family Allowances matters. This lad has his identification disc so there is no trouble placing him. He is wearing a parka issued on Family Allowances. December 10, 1950.

PHOTOGRAPH BY J.C. JACKSON — COURTESY OF THE NATIONAL ARCHIVES OF CANADA, PA102695 — INDIAN AND NORTHERN AFFAIRS COLLECTION.

Eskimo spearing Arctic char, fish trap, native encampment, Boothia Peninsula, N.W.T., Sept. 4, 1937.

PHOTOGRAPH BY D.L. MCKEAND — COURTESY OF THE NATIONAL ARCHIVES OF CANADA, PA102196 — INDIAN AND NORTHERN AFFAIRS COLLECTION.

We have a lot to learn if we are to undo the negative influences in our life. We have to laugh in the face of all dictatorships, both mental and physical. If they are divested of their power they will vanish.

AIRBORNE AGAIN

In August 1980 Reg Pfeiffer, an electronics engineer at Mitel Corporation, invited me to join him and his Uncle Harold on an extended flying expedition to the Canadian north and Alaska. Harold, an accomplished sculptor, was intending to meet and work with some native acquaintances. Reg, a very experienced pilot, would be flying his Cessna 185 (a four-seater, with high wings, on floats). He is a superb navigator and is licensed to fly with instruments, day or night, so I accepted his offer with enthusiasm.

As it worked out, we had three and a half weeks of glorious flying that allowed us to see many parts of Canada and Alaska that are usually inaccessible. We met native people from Great Slave Lake and Great Bear Lake in the Northwest Territories and across the border; we visited the Gwich'in Indian settlement of Fort Yukon and the Eskimo village of Unalakleet on Norton Sound in the Bering Sea in Alaska, and other natives at Anthony Island in the Queen Charlotte Islands; we flew over Indian settlements like Old Crow in the Yukon on the banks of the Porcupine River; we got a good look at huge forest fires; and we saw the immense clear-cutting of Canadian forests on Vancouver Island and the British Columbia mainland. Even the overflights of Northern Ontario, Manitoba, Saskatchewan, and Alberta revealed a completely different view of the land, showing us for instance how man has tried to push back the forests in Saskatchewan to gain more land for agriculture.

During the flight across the prairies we tested the capacity of the Cessna to take off with the three of us and our luggage. We had landed on Waskesiu Lake in Saskatchewan, north of Prince Albert, 2,000 feet above sea level. The thinner air at that elevation does not provide enough lift for a Cessna that is full of fuel, with an extra 20-gallon tank stowed behind the seats. We could not get airborne, so returned to the marina. Some of Uncle's heavy modelling clay was reloaded into the tips of the floats in order to shift the weight forward and get it off the heels of the floats so as to reduce their friction during takeoff.

A selection of our clothing was left behind, as well as some books. Some young Swiss travellers were delighted to get bags of dried fruit and other luxury food. The reorganization worked: we were airborne again.

We had the same problem on a small lake just outside Fort McMurray in Alberta. More food was dropped to folks we spied in a canoe. The voyageurs were delighted to lighten our larder. But that left almost no food for us. But Reg was a good fisherman, we thought, and we would be stopping at several spots known for fine fishing. Unfortunately, these spots didn't live up to their reputations.

One glorious day followed another, each with interesting and satisfying events.

One of the most important stops that Reg intended to make was Little Doctors Lake in the Northwest Territories, to visit with Gus Krause and

Aleut Sea Otter Hunters.

PHOTOGRAPH BY GUY F. CAMERON — COURTESY OF ALASKA AND POLAR REGIONS DEPT.
UNIVERSITY OF FAIRBANKS — BASSOC GLASS NEGATIVES — SELID, 6492517N.

his Indian wife Mary, who lived there in a log cabin. Theirs is a spectacular setting. Harold wanted to do sculptures of their heads. Gus Krause was a northern legend. Eighty-five years old and of German descent, he had left Chicago in 1917, settled as trapper and guide in the Nahanni region, and never left. We met him, his wife Mary, 68, and their granddaughter. We were greeted with smiles and good coffee and heard about Gus's correspondence courses in Spanish. He is working at keeping his brain active. What a guy!

When we left, we promised to return. Later that day we checked out a small glacier lake in Nahanni Park. We brought the plane down near — very near — Virginia Falls to wait out a storm that was brewing. We stayed only long enough to investigate the falls at ground level, then took off again to find a camping site for the night. Tea over an open fire and freeze-dried dinner tasted great. Breakfast was supposed to be fresh fish, but they did not cooperate with Reg. We checked out Watson Lake and spent some time at Muncho Lake in British Columbia, where my daughter Heike was working for the summer at the Highland Glen Lodge. We had celebrated her seventeenth birthday there in 1977. Frauke and Theo, the owners, had become good friends. Theo hailed from near my hometown and spoke Lower German fluently, as did I. That fabulous couple had even advertised "We snack ok platt!" in the MilePost (a fine guide for travel in the northwestern reaches of Canada and in Alaska). The language was music to my ears, and helped to establish our friendship, as did Heike's working there. We enjoyed the great feast they set out for us, but regrettably we had to get right back in the air to fly to Little Doctors Lake, where Mary and Gus Krause had pitched a tent for us.

Next morning, after I had a good swim in the rather cold lake to clear the cobwebs, we enjoyed a stack of pancakes and hot tea from Mary's kitchen, and Uncle got to work on a sculpture of Gus.

Our flight back the next day, toward Yellowknife again, was rather violent. A hot updraft from huge forest fires below buffeted our little plane. We climbed higher, but there too the air currents were violent, and the smell of smoke was intense.

From Yellowknife we made several excursions in search of good fishing that led to trouble landing and taking off in shallow or muddy water. I found myself having to jump in and out of freezing lakes to pull or guide the plane to get it airborne.

Finally, on a small lake outside Tuktoyaktuk, Reg caught some beautiful Arctic grayling. We had a feast at last, and it left us with smiling faces.

After our superb meal of pan-fried grayling, we crisscrossed the Mackenzie River delta. It was dazzling. I had never seen such an extensive waterway before. There were thousands of small streams, puddles, and lakes, with some larger channels meandering between them, as far as the eye could see, right out to the Beaufort Sea. Little did I know then that in April 1992 I would travel the ice road on that giant of a river, from Inuvik to Aklavik and Tuktoyaktuk.

When we entered Alaska at Fort Yukon, a charming customs lady came to our plane at the

In Curtis, E.S. The North American Indian (Norwood, Mass., 1930).

COURTESY OF THE NATIONAL ARCHIVES OF CANADA, C37116.

water's edge. We were on our way to Fairbanks, Alaska's second-largest city. The towering Alaska Range loomed mightily in the background. The Fairbanks airport is actually three facilities in one. There is a large commercial, international section, as well as a section not much smaller for lighter, mostly private planes and smaller carriers. I saw there for the first time an artificial "sea base" for float-equipped planes. Given Alaska's geography, there must be thousands of such versatile machines, including amphibious ones. It was quite a sight. Planes were coming and going at a steady pace. We even saw the famous, almost indestructible "Goose," which dates from the days of the Second World War.

Our next destination was Dawson City, where Hans Algotson and his wife Debbie, longtime Yukoners, she a teacher and he a carpenter, guide, and trapper, loaned us their truck to get around in. We met Karen Christie, another old friend, who had boarded Heike and me some years earlier, at Bear Creek, a famous golddigger's haunt. Northern hospitality sometimes seems to engulf one in a wonderful richness. It warms the heart and often also fills the stomach.

Karen Christie arranged for us to spend the night in the cabin of Bob and Julia Frisch, another example of northern generosity. Such human warmth, camaraderie, and genuine caring, together with the pull of the northern landscape, is what draws me back.

The might and power of the subarctic and Arctic landscape can bring us down to size. It can both elate and diminish us, with the wide-open spaces, the mountains and the sea, the tundra and taiga, the rivers and streams, the profusion of wildflowers in the spring and summer, the howling winds and snow and ice in winter. The light varies, from darkness, through long twilight hours, to sunshine that seems never to end.

But we had to return again to Alaska. It had become very hot and muggy. One could feel thunderstorms building up. We headed toward McKinley Park, now called Denali, the natives' word for "The Big One," Mount McKinley. An approaching wall of thunder and huge banks of clouds intervened. We spotted a small camp on the shores of Wein Lake, and dropped down on our floats. We had barely secured the plane, with the help of Dale Jensen, the camp's owner, who had come to greet us, when the clouds let go and deluged us with a formidable amount of wind-driven water. Dale's black retriever, Duck, greeted us at his cabin, where we met Beckey, a leftover guest from a previous fishing party. That party had left the day before with a load of guests and a big catch of fish. They had to choose between the fish and Beckey. She stayed. That's Alaska for you. Incredible and unique.

(Wakeham Expedition) Esquimaux, Douglas Harbour (P.Q.), Oct. 28, 1897.

PHOTOGRAPH BY GRAHAM DRINKWATER — COURTESY OF THE NATIONAL ARCHIVES OF CANADA, C84702 — WAKEHAM EXPEDITION COLLECTION.

Admirality Inlet skin tent encampment, July 1889.

PHOTOGRAPH BY WALTER LIVINGSTONE-LEARMONTH — COURTESY OF THE NATIONAL ARCHIVES OF CANADA, C88352 — LIVINGSTONE-LEARMONTH COLLECTION.

ON THE QUEEN CHARLOTTE ISLANDS

Later in our trip, after numerous landings and take-offs, some quite simple but several complicated by our unfamiliarity with the bodies of water we were using, we ended up pitching our tent on the deck of a bridge. It had been late when we decided to go down to a spot where the map indicated the loading dock of a peat moss plant. We found ourselves tangling with a bridge that got me out treading on the central rib of a wing, disengaging it from the wooden structure. I had to push with all my might against the powerful tidal current. But she seemed not to budge, though she was not going any farther under. So, slowly, very slowly, inch by inch, the wing was freed and the floats turned, now aided by the currents. The engine roared. Reg was in control once again. But he left me dangling from the bridge. It is amazing the power the human body can muster when willed to do so. I made it onto the deck of bridge, shaking in my boots.

That night we again pitched our tent on the bridge deck, made some grub for our growling stomachs, and soon we were snoring. (Reg was very good at that too.) It had been a very long day, from Whitehorse in the Yukon all the way down the Alaska Panhandle, with stopovers in Petersburg and Prince Rupert.

Toward the end of our flying excursion we visited Haida, Masset, Queen Charlotte Town, and Skidegate. Skidegate gave us a good idea of what it must have been like in centuries past, and Bill Reid's large new totem pole was very impressive. The next phase of island-hopping was by far the most memorable. We found a super spot for the night, where there was a sulphuric hot spring in a most beautiful setting. From the natural recess in a rock, made almost to human measure, into which the pleasantly warm water flowed, there was a view of a bay surrounded by tall trees and rocky shorelines. Out on the water a tall ship was at anchor. A light breeze, sunshine, and mild temperatures. All the cares of the world dropped away. It was manna for the soul as well as for the aching bones. To top it off, we had plenty of food. Huckleberries grew all around, ours for the picking. We had a campfire going well into the night. Paradise!

We dropped out of the sky onto Anthony Island. Another beautiful sunny day, with almost too much contrast for photography. A crew of Haida Indians and some non-native helpers were trying to clean up the old village site. The longhouses had collapsed into their pits. Everything was overgrown with vegetation. Mother nature had reclaimed the site.

We spent a few hours there with the Haidas. Their generosity and guidance provided another stepping stone that led to my current venture to try to make the voice of the natives heard.

When we returned to our plane we found it high and dry on the pebbles of the beach where we had

Eskimo in their kayaks, ca. 1901.

COURTESY OF THE NATIONAL ARCHIVES OF CANADA, C5106.

secured her. With logs as rollers and the help of our new friends we got her to float again. I was very sad to leave so soon. I was in the grip of the moment, the encounter, and the site. But the end of our journey was in sight. We had no definite timetable, but we all felt it.

Soon Vancouver Island was beneath us. Huge stretches of clear-cut came into view. We flew over a ravaged land. Nanaimo and Victoria were sighted below as we began our homeward journey. The flight through the mountains of the mainland — the Coastal range and then the Rockies — was incredible!

How puny the roads and railways, how minuscule the villages. What is man in such surroundings? The true scale of our importance was made clear to us.

An artificial lake 3,500 feet above sea level near Calgary was my last touchdown on this memorable trip. However, the next day the lake did not want to let go of the loaded plane. The air was too hot and humid. The water was like a mirror. No amount of rocking or going in circles to create our own waves for liftoff altered the fact that we were trying to trick nature into changing her laws just a little bit to let us go. All the engine's screaming and all our cursing did not help us one bit. The plane was overloaded or underpowered, or both. We were stuck.

Uncle Harold and I were dumped on shore and soon we lost sight of our little plane. Reg was in full control, by himself, probably chuckling, heading for

Waskesiu Lake to retrieve the cache we'd left three weeks earlier. We were supposed to follow, and the next day Uncle did. By 18:30 hours that same day I was back in Ottawa, via commercial jet. We had had an incredible three and a half weeks of flying, with only two days on the ground.

NUNAVUT OPTIMISM

The signing of the Agreement in Principle for the establishment of Nunavut was a benchmark in the renewal of confidence and self-esteem among northern natives. This truly historic event took place on 30 April 1990 in Igloolik, in what is known today as Nunavut, at that time part of the Northwest Territories. Igloolik is an island community of about 1,200 people, situated in the eastern Arctic about 150 kilometres north of the Arctic Circle, just off the northwestern tip of the Melville Peninsula.

In late April and early May there is almost

A view showing Topek (summer house), Kayak and Eskimo. Peel River, N.W.T., 1901.

PHOTOGRAPH BY C.W. MATHERS — COURTESY OF THE NATIONAL ARCHIVES OF CANADA, PA135821

24 hours of daylight at these latitudes, though there is still snow cover, and it is of course cold by southern Canadian standards. The flight from Ottawa was in two stages, first by jet to Iqaluit on Baffin Island and then to Igloolik by Twin Otter, the reliable workhorse airplane of the north. Accommodation was at a premium for this big event, since hordes of southerners attended to witness the signing of the Agreement and to take part in the merriment to follow. The signing was the culmination of years of negotiation between the Inuit and the Canadian federal government.

Plane after plane disgorged their human cargo — Indian and Northern Affairs Minister Tom Siddon, departmental deputies, negotiators, the press, hangers-on — into this isolated settlement. The ceremony itself took place in the school auditorium. The entire population had been invited to witness the event. I was moved by the proud faces of the Inuit, by the feeling of joy expressed in their eyes, and by certain remarks of a village elder, translated from his native Inuktitut. However, the signing by the politicians and their native counterparts, and the speeches, while legally important, were only one aspect of the occasion.

The mood was one of optimism, and that good feeling spilled over into the big community feast afterwards. The next day, when the community gathered together for outdoor activities, plays, games, and dogsled rides, the air was still charged with warmth and optimism. The largest igloo ever built was the site of traditional drum-dancing, performed with great abandon. It was a fabulous structure, evidence of the Inuit skill in utilizing whatever nature provides.

INTRODUCTION TO ALOOTOOK IPELLIE

John Amagoalik introduced me to Alootook Ipellie, an Inuk writer, poet, cartoonist, and photographer. Alootook served for close to ten years as editor of the magazine *Inuit Today*, the forerunner of *Inuktitut*. He is also president of the Baffin Island Writers' Trust. He has been actively struggling, in his own way, for his people. Like all Inuit, he is a sharp and keen observer, full of wit and quiet humour.

His essay provides insight into the traumatic, rapid changes that our society has forced on all natives. These changes have been far too sudden and severe not to cause very serious injury to the psyches of the affected people, rendering many of them unable to cope and susceptible to alcohol and drug abuse, and making it impossible for them to live normal lives. But he is positive and full of hope, true to his Inuit nature. **HB**

PEOPLE OF THE GOOD LAND

Alootook Ipellie

If the moralist is inclined to speculate on the nature and distribution of happiness in this world [let him consider the Eskimo]: a horde so small, so secluded, occupying so apparently helpless a country, so barren, so wild and so repulsive; and yet enjoying the most perfect vigour, the most well fed health.
— *John Ross, English explorer, 1830*

One hundred and sixty-three years after Captain John Ross wrote these words, a modern-day Arctic explorer can use the same words and still be close to explaining the truth about the nature of the Inuit and his environment. The only difference is that the modern-day explorer will find twentieth-century dwellings grouped together in small communities all across the circumpolar Arctic. Long gone are clusters of nomadic camps that once dotted the secluded, helpless country. To the naked eye, the land still seems barren and wild, and sometimes is considered repulsive when one is caught in the perfect vigour of the unpredictability of the harsh winter weather.

A well-fed health did bring happiness to the Inuit, as it does today, but the horde is still small in comparison to the burgeoning population of the world. If today's moralist is to speculate about the nature and happiness of the present-day Inuit, he is bound to be a little surprised by what history has done to them ever since that day in 1830.

The element of nature does not take kindly to the inhabitants of the Arctic, or to those who visit and spend time in it. That is why it is respected by all human beings like a kindly, old grandfather — for its gentleness, but mainly for its fury. Many have perished in it, some forgotten forever, since there was no one around to acknowledge their deaths. Nature in the Arctic is like that, uncaring one moment, then lavishing love with its many-splendoured beauty. No wonder it has a way of controlling the behaviour and psychology of its inhabitants.

Over the centuries, the availability of different animal species spawned distinctive fashion apparel crafted by some of history's best seamstresses. What can one say about the integrity of those who designed the hunting tools of survival in an unrepenting land? We will not rest easy until recognition is bestowed on those who invented tools and weapons designed to function in a precise way. Who among us does not marvel at the intricate beauty and resourcefulness of an ulu, the woman's knife?

These are some of the qualities that make Inuit unique among cultures in this world. Even though they live in one of the world's most inhospitable climates, their enduring characteristic is a people warm of heart who are always ready to help anyone struggling with life. If the art of human relations were to be measured among all peoples on the planet, Inuit would score high on a list of those who are experts in caring for his fellow man. This is not surprising given the fact they have always relied on one another to survive the unpredictable forces of nature.

Another positive aspect of their culture is their oral tradition. Before the arrival of the "Qallunaat" (white people), most adults acquired the wonderful ability to recite the tales and legends of their great land. This was a natural product of a culture that revels in the game of story-telling marathons during long winter nights. These marathons were interpersed with traditional games, drum dances, chanting, and song-duelling. The main purpose of

Lady with tobacco pipe – group of Indian or Eskimo? women in front of log building. Churchill? Man. 1909.

PHOTOGRAPH BY GEORGE REID MUNRO – COURTESY OF THE NATIONAL ARCHIVES OF CANADA, PA147461 – GEORGE REID MUNRO COLLECTION.

numbers of each species they hunted throughout different seasons. This practice ensured the survival of as many species as possible when the short spring and summer brought thousands of newborn to the grounds of various Arctic sanctuaries. Apart from being lifelong hunters and gatherers, Inuit were devout conservationists. It was always in their best interest not to kill off any species of animals to extinction. To do so would mean they would be helping themselves commit a slow suicide as a distinct entity within a world cultural mosaic.

BRUTE BEASTS

"These savages were clothed in beasts skins, and did eat raw flesh, and spoke such speech, that no man could understand them, and their demeanour, were like the brute beasts."

So spoke Italian explorer John Cabot, speaking of three Inuit he brought back to England in 1494. One can imagine what the Europeans may have thought of the Inuit who were brought back to their soil from the alien world that was the Arctic at that time.

These "savages" were indeed different, "like brute beasts." They were aliens in a so-called civilized world. They were treated as curios, because they were considered to be like other museum pieces — live archeological displays. They were no doubt carefully scrutinized by hundreds upon thou-

creating stories and legends was to entertain. Some stories had practical purposes and were used as teaching tools for young children. Living within an oral tradition meant that each generation had to hand down the language and the culture by word of mouth. This also meant that most Inuit needed the ability to retain detail, even the most minute descriptions, about certain things that were important to their continued survival. Failure to do so might mean serious injury, or fatality. The harsh Arctic climate had no feeling for even the most well-prepared men and women as they travelled the vast land.

The traditional Inuit also needed to be a visual people if they hoped to survive in the Arctic. They had to possess a keen memory, and record in their mind's eye the varying landscapes they encountered each day. So, as they moved from an old hunting ground to a new one, they learned that certain areas

became special places for different reasons. A particular coastal area might become known for its abundance of edible berries and plants. Another area inland was an age-old caribou migrating route. A group of islands in a fjord was a resting place for walrus herds. Another part beyond a peninsula was a nesting ground for eider ducks. A great river in a beautiful valley was a lifeline to schools of Arctic char.

Once certain areas of the land were recognized for their varying vegetation, and characteristics such as whether or not there was an abundance of a particular wildlife species, they were often marked with Inukshuit — stone cairns — resembling human beings. Many a landmark, river or lake, was given a name for the purpose of identification, so that, as the seasons changed, they were returned to, because of their abundance in seasonal game or certain types of flora and fauna. This resulted in the preservation of

Group of Inuit. (Left to right at right): Abel, Joshua. Hopedale, Labrador, August 1886.

COURTESY OF THE NATIONAL ARCHIVES OF CANADA, PA139027 — PINKNEY, WILLIAM AND LOIS.

sands of smirky faces with piercing eyes. They must have lived their last days in a circus-like atmosphere. They probably had no choice but to return the amusement of so many odd characters who went to see them each day.

The downside to all this was that the Inuit contracted diseases from the very public who came in droves to see and admire them. Without immunity to these diseases, the so-called "savages" were, in their demeanour, not like brute beasts any more. They became humiliated individuals who soon turned into confused, purposeless human vegetables. Indeed, "they spoke such speech, that no man [in Europe] could understand them."

Herein lies their eventual undoing. None of us who are their descendants can doubt they spoke endlessly of wanting to go back to their homeland, to their paradise, and to their people, family and friends, as well as to their companions, their daily diet, and the pursuit of happiness on their sacred land. But no Europeans listened to their heart-felt yearnings,

Representative of the Department of Indian Affairs S.J. Bailey explaining the benefits of pablum to two Inuit women with babies. Repulse Bay, N.W.T., 1948.

PHOTOGRAPH ATTRIBUTED BY S.J. BAILEY — COURTESY OF THE NATIONAL ARCHIVES OF CANADA, PA167631 — INDIAN AND NORTHERN AFFAIRS COLLECTION.

ever by losing its virginity to professional exploiters from all over the globe.

In time, Canada and the United States of America began to identify their respective international borders. Both countries would eventually claim all the land within those borders, despite the fact that the aboriginals had lived there from time immemorial.

Then these colonizers decided that the nomadic Inuit were ripe to be assimilated to the larger, dominant societies. They were eventually to make sure that the full power of their tax dollars would be spent helping to re-make an indigenous culture into something very similar to their own. The immediate aim was to make it easier for the Inuit to be ministered to as well as to administrate.

This was the beginning of their wholesale attempt at "civilizing" the brute beasts.

My generation is the realization of that great attempt, although the colonizers did not have the means to change our biological inheritance or to manipulate our psychological make-up. It is a wonder that they did not systematically brainwash each newborn to conform to their way of dealing with this world. We remain forever grateful for this oversight. But the ugly reality today is the legacy of the administrators who were given the authority to begin manipulating our lives so that we would one day abandon our culture and language. "Big Brother" has been in the Arctic for a long time. "Thought Control" was never very far behind.

because none of them understood their language.

These three Inuit were among others who also had their lives stolen by thieves who appointed themselves "guest curators" to a curious European public. It must have been humbling for them to die so horribly as the disease crept into their bodies, disease that was still alien back in their homeland.

It would not be unreasonable to speculate that their skeletal remains were retained to be later put inside glass display cases for the public to ponder about and compare bone structures with. Even

in their death, these unfortunate souls were not allowed to rest in peace. How much more humiliation could they be shown by a curious "civilized" world? Later European contact demonstrated the exploitation of these "brute beasts" in other ways. As the vast Arctic began to be frequented by fur traders and whalers, and then colonized, it seemed that all the Arctic had in renewable and non-renewable resources was simply up for grabs. Inuit cultural upheaval was just around the corner. The pristine Arctic was about to change for-

A.P. Low Expedition – Natives dressed for Dance, Fullerton, Hudson Bay, 1904. Left to right: Hattie and Jennie.

PHOTOGRAPH BY J.D. MOODIE – COURTESY OF THE NATIONAL ARCHIVES OF CANADA, C1826 – R.C.M.P. COLLECTION.

LIVING IN TWO WORLDS

Big Brother and Thought Control crept into Inuit lives like the plague in the early part of this century. They moved across the Arctic like giant bulldozers. Nothing could stop them from pushing their way into the lives of the nomadic Inuit. I, too, felt the thrust of these bulldozers one fateful day when they arrived at our hunting camp.

We were soon forced to move, along with many other families, to Iqaluit, a small coastal community on southern Baffin Island. I still have vivid memories of those heady days when we did not hunt anymore to support ourselves. Instead we began relying on canned food and dried goods sold from a local Hudson's Bay Company store. We scavenged wood from the dump and built our huts in clusters, away from the modern pre-fab houses of the Qallunaat. Often we went to the same dump to supplement our diet and sometimes found usable household utensils. And, if we were lucky on any given day, we also found used clothing thrown away by the privileged Qallunaat.

It wasn't until some years later that we found out the real reason why we had been moved to Iqaluit. The government had made it mandatory for all school-age children to start attending school. It touched on absurdity. The parents ended up tagging along just so their children could enter the academic world. Their status as heads of families was diminished, because the principals and the teachers had the sole authority to teach Inuit children whatever was on the curriculum. As a student participant, I got a glimpse of the Qallunaat world in my studies. But not a single subject was devoted to my culture and language.

Looking back, it seems that most of us were blind to what was really happening around us. Those who had some inkling feigned approval, hoping it would be for the better. At least our people would not have to struggle on the land anymore as they once did when animals became scarce or when the weather didn't co-operate. This was a way of avoiding godawful famines or starvation. What people would not extend its empty hands for live-saving essentials like food, shelter, and clothing, or would refuse modern medicine to combat certain diseases that they had no immunity to? Since these essentials were in the hands of authority — the government workers and administrators — they had no choice but to succumb to leading a very different life than they were used to.

The government workers and administrators should be given kudos for devising a system of subtle assimilation of a whole people in broad daylight! I have to admit to being blind to what was happening to us.

Because of their material wealth and modern technology, the Qallunaat seemed to have a superior society. I too was attracted to their colourful world, their sweet food, and the ingenuity with which they had invented toys for a modern world. Some of these toys included devices for entertaining whole Inuit families, whose own cultural heritage was rapidly being superseded by the likes of gramophones, radios, and film reels. Certainly they helped us to dump our centuries-old traditional games and to discontinue learning the art of telling tales and legends, and eventually stopped us from occasionally creating our songs of joy and sorrow. As we gained knowledge of this new world, we were able to learn to speak, read, and write English. We were uprooting ourselves from the very land that had borne and bred us. We weren't speaking our language as well as our ancestors had and hunted less the good animals of the land. We did not seek out

Inuit transporting supplies for RCMP from *C.D. Howe*. Pangnirtung, N.W.T., July 1951.

PHOTOGRAPH BY WILFRED DOUCETTE — COURTESY OF THE NATIONAL ARCHIVES OF CANADA, PA146649 — NATIONAL FILM BOARD OF CANADA.

advice from the wisdom of our elders, as we had done out on the land and in our hunting camps. They, too, were being victimized by the rapidity of change in our midst.

The snowball, so to speak, was rolling down the mountain, picking up victims as it got bigger, and even bigger. No one, it seemed, was ever going to be able to stop this snowball from continuing down the mountain. And for years this was true. The powers-that-be were perfectly content to play the spectator, oblivious to the catastrophe they had initiated, intended or not.

FROZEN IN THE SNOW

One of the most vivid memories of my childhood was a rumour that started going around in our community that a woman had been found totally naked,

Niviatsianaq, or Shoofly, seated before her sewing-machine in the winter deck house on the *Era*; photographed by Captain George Comer.

REGISTRARS OFFICE, MYSTIC SEAPORT MUSEUM INC. MYSTIC, CONNECTICUT 06355 — COMER COLLECTION.

half buried in the Arctic snow. I did not know how to react to this rumour, since she was not a member of our immediate family. The woman must have died suffocating in the fury of nature's wrath, gasping for the last bit of air, or, failing that, simply looked death in the face and peacefully closed her eyes for the last time. Death, even in its ugliness, was welcome to this woman, if only because it ended her agony in the final seconds before she went to sleep. However, it was the real cause of her death that was most telling about the dilemma the Inuit in our community were facing: alcohol abuse and its related problems.

Alcoholism was a new social disease with no ready cure, because it was such an unknown quantity. In the beginning, those who started drinking drank only to get drunk — and in their drunkenness, abused members of their families and others in the community. Some were simply victims of over-indulgence, like the woman found naked in the snow. In the months and years that followed, she would not be the only such victim, as I had hoped.

I sometimes observed the drunkards' argumentative inclinations and the inevitable brawls that often caused permanent scars and irreparable bodily harm. These few initial quarrels seemed tame when compared to the mental and spiritual injury inflicted on those who abused alcohol. However, the ugliest face of alcoholism arrived when people began shooting and knifing each other in order to solve some argument, which was often left inconclusive with the death of one or the other. The fury of the human mind, drugged to accept violence as if it were normal human behaviour in a "civilized" setting, became quite common in our community.

Some civic-minded people started asking questions about the growing problem of alcohol abuse. What to do about something that had been totally foreign only a few short years before? How to amend the type of human suffering we had never seen before? How to educate a people about the effects of alcohol, when it was already too late? Who to turn to when one was caught in a cycle of no return? How to prevent another tragedy when one didn't have the know-how to help alleviate the escalation of violent death among our innocent populace? Questions without answers. The tragedies of the future could not be prevented in a reasonable way.

I felt as helpless as the next person. I only ended up participating in this tragedy as one of the victims. I cried out but no one noticed, since they didn't have the means or the tools to help me either.

A CULTURAL WHITEOUT

As an Inuk living in the Arctic, you can expect to get trapped in a whiteout several times each winter. The cultural upheaval we experienced in our community in the late 1950s and early 1960s seemed in retrospect a lot like being caught in a whiteout — trapped and unable to go forward since you could not see clearly where you were heading. So, our society had to rely on another society to be the guide dog to our blind culture. Some individuals were luckier than others, since they could use a cane to help them make some progress — one step at a time. Those who did not have a cane to guide them soon lost themselves in a whirlpool of no return. No new dawn gave evidence that things were going to turn around for the better even as the Inuit culture screamed in agony. Who or what was going to save this infant in distress? In the end the cultural whiteout would not lift for many more years.

The transitional period from hunters and gatherers to community dwellers took some time to evolve. This was the period that proved fatal for many Inuit, who, for various personal reasons, could not readily adjust. For many families it was a time of uncertainty, as they diligently tried so to adopt a new lifestyle and met only failure. Many individuals became suspended in midstream, unable to go along with the flow or to fight against it. The situation verged on social chaos.

The colonial social reformers — if they were not surprised by the turn of events — would deny full responsibility for the socio-cultural unrest in the communities. Their "cure" for whatever was ailing the Inuit was to put more money in. The powers-that-be had unwittingly opened a Pandora's box. So

Angulalik shows the results of his trading. Perry River, N.W.T.

PHOTOGRAPH BY J.C. JACKSON — COURTESY OF THE NATIONAL ARCHIVES OF CANADA, PA102701 — INDIAN AND NORTHERN AFFAIRS COLLECTION.

they had to be grateful for living in a rich country that could afford to fork out millions of dollars each fiscal year to try to put a lid back on the box. But all the money spent on the new social problems did not guarantee easy solutions. And that has been proven to be true to this very day.

ACADEMIC TOILS AND SPOILS

Looking back to where I came from and how I was raised, I am extremely proud of my Inuit heritage. Perhaps I can try to illuminate why this is so. I think it's important that a member of any cultural group should be enlightened enough to interpret what is happening to his or her people in a given era or generation. It is impossible for me to know exactly what is going through the minds of my fellow Inuit in this day and age. However, I can offer a synopsis, from my own perspective.

Most of us have an idea about our people's prehistory and know our recent recorded history to the present day. These have been mulled over hundred and thousands of times by historians as well as by ordinary people who have an interest in the subject. So let me begin my synopsis from 1951, the year I was born, in a hunting camp on Baffin Island.

I have heard from my mother, and other close relatives who were at my birth, that I was so small they all thought I would never make it to the next moment or the next day. Delicate as I must have been, I persevered and survived. I spent my first few years as part of a semi-nomadic family, travelling from camp to camp, following wild game. I was to find out later in my youth that my father had died in a hunting accident before I was even one year old. So it must have been a difficult time for my mother, who struggled to keep me alive while mourning the unexpected death of my father. Life can play a cruel game with human beings.

My earliest memories of Iqaluit have to do with living in a hut in the wintertime and then moving into a tent from the start of spring until early fall. Most of the Inuit families who had moved to the community did the same. We simply could not stand living in a dark hut when we could enjoy so much light inside the white canvas tents. These seasonal rituals slowly died when the government began building pre-fabricated houses for all Inuit families. So each year the numbers of the Inuit-built huts dwindled, until one day the last one was torn down. We were well on our way to living in a semi-modern world as set out by government workers and administrators. It was during the same time that we were slowly forgetting and abandoning our distinct way of doing things and looking at the world. On the other hand, unbeknownst to many of us, it was being taken away from us. Our world would never be the same as it had been.

Like my childhood friends, I was suddenly immersed in a one-room school, which was also the Anglican church. It was inside this room that I began to learn about a world that might as well have been on another planet. It was not long before I found out exactly where our teacher came

"King-nuck" son of "At-ang–e-la" in princely pose.

PHOTOGRAPHED BY GERALDINE MOODIE AT FULLERTON, 1905 — PHOTO CREDIT TO THE R.C.M.P. MUSEUM — REGINA, SASK.

from and that our people were not the only people living on this planet after all, as we had thought. We were rapidly losing our virginity as a culture without really knowing this was happening.

The Qallunaat immersion program rooted itself deeper when I was selected as one of two Inuit students from our school to be sent to Ottawa for higher education. Here I was, a total stranger to a large city, being put into a Qallunaat home to live for the next ten months of the year. The first few weeks in Ottawa I felt as if I was being put through a wringer while riding a high-speed train. It turned out to be an emotional roller-coaster ride.

I remember coming out of the plane at Montreal on the first leg of my trip to Ottawa. It felt as if I had just entered a quasi-inferno. I will never forget how hot the wind felt on my face. It reminded me of the little 45-gallon oil drum we used to have for a furnace in our hut in Iqaluit. We would always huddle around it in order to keep warm in the dead of winter. It turned out to be a very hot first few days. The sweat that poured from my scalp and down to my toes proved it. It was the first time in my life that I begged for a cool Arctic summer breeze to slap my face.

I was still a naive young adult, and it was a great struggle for me to get used to the Qallunaat way of doing things. I was given no room to slacken off my studies as I had been able to back home in Iqaluit. This was an added pressure I could not avoid. So I had no choice but to tough-sled it if I wanted to survive my first year in the south and continue to acquire higher education.

I was overwhelmed by how enormous everything around me was. The Qallunaat couldn't do anything small-scale. Even if they knew how, they were not going to touch it with a hundred-foot pole. The reality was all around me: endless roads, endless highrises and houses, endless human beings. At first, dealing with the endless numbers was a little scary; then I began to look at it as a challenge. This turned out to be the secret to my survival in an urban jungle.

Back home, it was easier dealing with my fellow Inuit, because they were of the same cultural background and language. In the Qallunaat world, I found it hard to speak the language, because I was not yet fluent in it and so was shy about speaking it. I kept this to myself for a long time, until the family I boarded with as well as my teachers at school reported to my Northern Affairs counsellors that I had great difficulty communicating with them.

This soon caused concern among those who had sponsored me so that I could get a higher education. They began warning me there was a possibility I would not be sent back south next school year if I did not start communicating with people. I was forced to promise them that I would make a better effort to speak to those around me.

Over time, this situation never really improved, so my counsellors concocted a plan to send me to a shrink! Each day after school at 4 o'clock I would go to the Royal Ottawa, a mental hospital, for a one-hour session. I would be stuck in a room with a strange woman who asked numerous questions that were never answered. Was I a bit deranged? No one ever found out, because they soon gave up trying to make me utter even a few words in English.

It was soon after this experience that I decided my report card would do the speaking for me. By the end of my first year in Ottawa I had passed grade 7 and 8, and was graciously invited back the next year.

Before I entered High School I really did not have any idea what I wanted to take. It was my art teacher who suggested I try vocational arts, since I had shown enough promise during my art classes. I took it upon myself to have the privilege of taking on the onerous world of the arts, which I soon got to love so much. At the young age of sixteen, I wasn't much of an artist, but I was convinced this was something perfectly suited to me and something I wanted to do for the rest of my life. My Northern Affairs counsellors, a little mystified by my career choice, tried to discourage me. Their preference was for me to take a trade that would be practical back in my hometown, like heavy equipment operator or office clerk. But I told them my mind was made up, and they reluctantly allowed me the freedom of choice.

I knew then that one day I would become a famous artist like the grandmasters we learned about in art class. I wanted so much to imitate them and tried hard to do so when I began the four-year Vocational Arts Course.

For a year and a half I toiled along with my fellow art students.

It was just before Christmas that I began to get homesick and started slacking off in my studies. One day I told my counsellors I could no longer devote my energies to my school work and that I was quitting. They immediately began asking me numerous questions, wanting to know exactly why I was giving up a great opportunity. They tried hard to convince me to stay to the end. I stuck to my guns and they finally gave up on me. I had had enough of Ottawa and its rigid timetables. I wanted to be free like the birds, coming and going as I pleased.

Once I was back in my hometown, it turned out to be a mixed blessing. I could not find any work and bided my time lounging around — bored out of my skull. I wanted to be back in Ottawa, but it wasn't as easy as picking my nose. My only recourse was to enrol in upgrading classes at the Adult

(A.P. Low Expedition) The *Era* perparing for spring whaling, Fullerton, (N.W.T.), May 1904.

PHOTOGRAPH BY A.P. LOW — COURTESY OF THE NATIONAL ARCHIVES OF CANADA, PA38270 — GEOLOGICAL SURVEY OF CANADA COLLECTION

Education Centre. This was one way of preventing my brain from vegetating. I also hoped that it would be my ticket back to Ottawa and what had been, at times, my beloved art classes. However, when the next school year began, I was one of a group of Iqaluit students selected to be sent to Yellowknife to complete my high school. Once there, I hated living in the student hostel and asked to go back to Ottawa. Miraculously, they listened to me! I was on my way to Ottawa during Christmas break.

I had become used to living in a big city, and Ottawa was a comfortable place to be. I began meet-ing new friends and spent time with other Inuit students, who were there for the same reasons as I. As welcome as the familiar sights were, my counsellors told me I could not go back to taking vocational arts. Their reasons for this were not clear to me, but I had a sneaky feeling they were still hoping to turn me into a heavy equipment operator or an office clerk. They reminded me that someone like me could not make a living in the arts, especially in the Arctic. I was put into a regular academic high school program. Shortly thereafter, I was disillusioned with it. Grade 10 High School would see the last of me and I headed back to Iqaluit once more. A failure in academics, I was a perfect candidate to be a failure in the job market. With this realization, I had made another blunder.

INUIT ASPIRATIONS THROUGH THE WRITTEN WORD

I was not going to let my academic failure stop me from dreaming. I managed to get a job with CBC Radio in Iqaluit as an announcer-producer. The pay

Group of Fullerton children.

PHOTOGRAPH BY A.P. LOW — COURTESY OF THE NATIONAL ARCHIVES OF CANADA, PA53577 — GEOLOGICAL SURVEY OF CANADA COLLECTION.

was good but the shift work was hard on me. The hours from 4 p.m. to 2 a.m. didn't turn out to be my cup of tea. My superior would promise to change my shifts but never went through with it. I began missing work and, after three months, was dismissed.

Back in Ottawa, I hung out at the national headquarters of the Inuit Tapirisat of Canada (ITC). ITC was a fledgling operation. They were publishing a small newsletter, *Inuit Monthly*, edited by an Inuk from my hometown. Having heard that I could draw and write poetry, he asked me to submit some work. In the end, he published one of my drawings on the cover of the newsletter and, inside, a poem! My long-held dream of being paid for my art and writing had come true. It was a revelation of sorts that encouraged me to keep up with what little talent I had. I started hanging out often enough at ITC that I ended up being commissioned to do six pen and ink drawings for their office. This allowed me to continue meeting my rent at a rooming house and stay in Ottawa.

One day, an opening for a translator with *Inuit Monthly* was advertised and I applied for and got it. I finally had a full-time job, which turned out to be tedious at first, but rewarding whenever an issue I had worked on came out. Even though I was only translating the fighting words created by other writers and ITC lawyers, I felt as if I was part of a team that was pushing hard for the rights of all Inuit in Canada. That was enough to kindle a small spark inside of me that seemed real, and I was determined to hang on, to participate in the fight of the century on behalf of my people. My initial employment as a translator became a spawning ground for my limited writing and artistic abilities. What I had learned in Vocational Arts was being put to practice when I started illustrating reports and stories, and drawing cartoon fillers.

My first writing project was a monthly serial

about my childhood experience in Iqaluit called "Those Were the Days." Writing this serial turned out to be both therapeutic and a learning process, since I began expressing some of the innermost feelings I had kept to myself throughout childhood and during my adolescence. The first time I understood the power of the written word was when readers began to respond to my writings.

CARRYING THE NUNAVUT TORCH

Our role as the staff of *Inuit Today* magazine was to publicize the goals and objectives of ITC. Most Inuit at that time were largely naive about politics and how they worked. We made it a point to help Inuit of Nunavut express their views and opinions about political decisions that were being made on their behalf. When I became a principal writer, I began writing articles on diverse subjects, including those on political, social, and cultural issues. It was an uncertain period for Inuit, since most of the communities were caught in the middle of a cultural upheaval.

Part of my duty was to explain some of the options open to the populace in a rapidly changing society. I did this in several ways: by writing timely editorials, essays, short stories, poetry, and articles, and by anchoring these with editorial/political cartoons. When these produced a response from the people, Inuit and non-Inuit, I knew that I was fulfilling my personal goal as an interpreter of Inuit concerns in order to bring about dialogue between Inuit, the government, and mainstream society in the south. I was determined not to relinquish such an important duty as long as I was needed. So I forged on, and became editor of the magazine close to ten years after I had started as a struggling translator.

It certainly was not an easy journey to my final arrival at the editorial position. In the intervening years, I had had an opportunity to visit many communities in the Arctic. I spoke with Inuit willing to share their views about current affairs, whether these covered politics, social issues, or language and culture. It was important to be on top of issues by keeping a constant watch on the pulse of public opinion. We could not afford to give up on what we were trying to achieve, for the good of our people and their children's future. Our leaders were about to begin negotiations with various levels of government to begin reclaiming what had been lost to our former colonizers.

No one doubted that it would take years, perhaps decades, to conclude successful negotiations. The last twenty years have proven this to be true. Looking back to that time, it was odd to watch the descendants of an ancient culture adapting to behavioural and psychological patterns employed by the dominant society. This adaptation was necessary if Inuit were to successfully nurture a relationship that could not be stopped. It was either make this relationship work or take a greater chance of losing everything to a much more politically powerful group. Inuit could not afford to play spectator as twentieth-century realities got a foothold in every community in the Arctic. They knew it was impossible to turn back the clock. They had to play the political game if they hoped ever to be on an equal footing with these veterans of the political profession. They learned at the beginning of their political careers that it was not going to be a cakewalk. So they prepared themselves to take a few lickings periodically and to roll with the punches as they came. This was not so different from dealing with the unpredictable forces of nature. They were determined to put on the political gloves as if they had worn them for centuries instead of mere decades.

TODAY'S ARCTIC IS ALIVE AND WELL

Inuit live in a magnificent part of the world — a natural refuge largely ignored over many centuries by the rest of humanity. The secret of its physical beauty is a secret no more. For millenniums it remained a sanctuary for many indigenous animal species and those that make seasonal migrations during its short summers. It is a sacred place for these animals as well as for the Inuit. While it is resource-rich, its ecology is one of the most fragile in the world. The land, the animals, and the Inuit are inseparable and their relationship seems to have been made in heaven. This is a reality that has never been properly understood by the dominant society. For this reason Inuit have much to teach others in other lands about the land's culture and heritage. They have to continue to put forward the message that it is the fragile Arctic ecology and its animals that help retain peace within their hearts and minds, and their spirituality. So it is important that they be given the power and authority by the dominant society to forge the future of their inherited domain, since they are in the best position to preserve it.

If there are nay-sayers out there, let them recognize this need by empowering the Inuit, so that the pristine and fragile land will be handled with the best of care, as if it was a newborn baby. The Inuit alone have understood its delicate nature in the past and will continue to do so in the future.

We Inuit refer to our homeland as "Paradise on Earth," and we know what we are speaking of.

WAKING UP

Alootool Ipellie

Waking up
Just as I have
In the last one hundred years
Barely ahead of the trickling-in of dawn

But this time there was a difference

A rude awakening
Had to blink a few times
To make sure the image stayed the same
After each opening of my lids

Then pinched both my cheeks
Slapped them slightly
To neutralize the tinge of pain
Spreading it around more evenly
So they would survive the ordeal

Stood up and looked down at my naked feet
Wanting to be re-assured
That they were indeed firmly planted
On the earth bound moss

Affirmation was there for the taking
If only I could find it
Within this misty soul

Turned around in despair
Hoping to see familiar faces
Afraid of what I might see
In the pre-dawn shadows
I became terrified of whatever
I had just turned away from
Scared of the unknown

Premature arrival of Armageddon
Just like being trapped in a nightmare
Running slightly ahead of certain death
The passage of time lasting forever

Who said waking up
Each morning was a blessing from god
For having survived another night
And again facing the un-doing
Of your consciousness

Life is like night and day
Painted in black and white
Graphic as ever
Does it mean we are headed for paradise
Or doomed to oblivion

That's the beauty of our lives
It is what keeps us going forward
Wondering
Wondering what is next to come
Around the next bend
Beyond the next horizon
By experiencing the unravelling of events
Within the edge of our vision
And in the universe of our minds

Waking up
From what was literally
A nomadic lifestyle the night before
To a lifestyle where Inuit hunters
Spend all their precious time
Sitting in front of a computer
Pushing predetermined buttons and keys
That allow them to launch
Rocket-powered harpoon missiles
Arrows and fish-spears

These are the days of return to innocence
Since the fish birds and animals
Never get to encounter
Their predatory enemies anymore

The Arctic has become a classless society
Since the tools of the twenty-first century
Have finally arrived

No pride nor dignity in that
And I am saddened
Since I cannot show off my skills anymore
To my loved ones
As well as to those who are accustomed
To being impressed
By my prowess as a great hunter

Waking up
Not needing to go outdoors to meet nature
As I was able to only yesterday

Damn

I had to work hard for my living
And I could also reward myself
With a triumphant kill
After having witnessed
The frightened eyes of

The bountiful bull caribou
The majestic polar bear
The sleek-backed ringed seal
The lumbering girth of a walrus
The feathered friend of a waterfowl
The slippery skin of an arctic char
And the welcome sight of a beluga whale

Waking up
Sitting in front of a damn computer
Breathing only used oxygen
Remembering my glory days
As a powerful shaman

Lament my friends and enemies
Lament for the enlightened days of yesterday
Lament for the husky who is forced to retire
Lament for the beautiful Arctic landscape
Which will never again be seen with naked eyes
Lament for the salty sea
For it will no longer hug me and my kayak
Lament for the sun and the moon
For they will no more show off their shine
Lament for the northern lights
For they will no more find human heads
To play ball with
Lament for the great spirit
Which takes care of the natural world
For its time has come to an end

Waking up
With a slap in the face

My preference is to go back to yesterday
And begin all over again

Tonight
I will think twice about going to sleep
I will be afraid of
Waking up

Group of Little White Whale Esquimaux playing their National Game of Ball (P.Q.).

PHOTOGRAPH BY GEORGE SIMPSON MCTAVISH — COURTESY OF THE NATIONAL ARCHIVES OF CANADA, C75911 — SIR SANDFORD FLEMING COLLECTION.

INTRODUCTION TO ARMAND TAGOONA

Armand Tagoona was the first Inuk to become an ordained priest, but subsequently found Christianity incompatible with Inuit values and traditions. He wrote this small essay, for which I have David Webster to thank, in April 1991, while living in Rankin Inlet, on the west side of Hudson Bay. Following the essay is an exchange of correspondence — between me and Justice J.E. Richards of the Supreme Court of the Northwest Territories — which is an account of the Armand Tagoona court case, his conviction, and his subsequent, tragic death. **HB**

THE HISTORY OF MY FOREFATHERS

Armand Tagoona

I do not know all of the history of my forefathers, so I will not be able to write everything. I do know the lifestyles of the people today; the lifestyles of our forefathers were very different. No one can live in one specific way forever. Sometimes without trying, people change. Even the earth is changing; you'll find that eating habits are changing, which causes the migration routes to change. Animals such as the caribou never used to approach an obvious camping ground or a community, because they were afraid, but now you will find that animals are able to get closer to communities than before, not only the caribou but also the fox, the polar bear, birds like geese and owls, and small birds. Snow birds and hunting birds have always been in the community.

Habits that were obviously Inuit habits are slowly changing. We are finding that people's eating habits are changing, our clothing styles are changing, and our sources of transportation are changing (from dogs to vehicles). We use trucks, snow-machines, motorboats — vehicles that can carry larger loads. Today's lifestyle is much more worrysome than the lifestyle of the past. The population is growing in such small areas. This is known by many people. Many people are going on vacations to areas where it is quiet and not busy, and where there is nothing to worry about.

My father's father's father lived a league out on the barren lands, lived off the wildlife and the country, and supported his wives and children off their land. If a man wanted more than one wife that was up to the man. Today a man can only have one wife, but we know of people today who, although they have one wife, live like they have two or three wives, because aside from the wife to whom the man is married, the man will also have lovers. Why? Because only one is tiring and boring. A person once said, "A man who is not married is more married than the man who is married."

My mother's mother's mother could choose to have more than one husband if she wanted to. She could be a second wife to one man if she agreed to. That choice was left to her. She could also agree to share her husband, but today that is not allowed. We also know of women today who, although they are married, have lovers. Why? Because just like the men, they are bored. Our lifestyle today is not much different from the lifestyle of our ancestors when it comes to things that were kept secret. The desires of the flesh are the same today as they were in past years.

Our ancestors lived in igloos in the winter and in tents made of caribou and sometimes sealskins in the summer. Both the igloo and the tent were round; igloos or tents were never square. When the white man arrived, square tents and houses were seen for the first time.

The world is round, the head of a person is round, the earth, human beings, wildlife, and all that was created are almost always round — the sun, the moon, the stars, all of these are round. When an Inuk "Eskimo" leaves a round igloo and enters a square house, he gets a headache and starts to worry. The man now has rules to abide by: "You are to do this, and don't do that." This creates headaches and worries.

Our ancestors did not have perfect lives. At times they starved, many died of diseases, large numbers at a time, died of accidents and mishaps, falling into the water or being attacked by wild animals, sometimes murdered over family disputes or marriage problems. Sometimes children would be physically or emotionally abused to the point of death. Sometimes babies would be thrown out, especially baby girls, because they would not make good hunters. Yes, our ancestors were not perfect during famines; you would find that people would get angry and jealous, because there was so little food.

Our ancestors had a much better attitude about life and got along very well among their own people. Relatives — husbands and wives, sisters-in-law or brothers-in-law, cousins — would call each other by their titles. Today you will find that people use each other's names instead, although many use titles.

Although our ancestors would never say "I love you" outright, love was often shown through works. Perhaps by giving furs and food to people in need. Also, if a man could not find a wife, a wife was given to him, and the same for the woman. Today money is used, and rather than sharing, people now have to ask for things. Sometimes families are forced to ask for meat when it should be given, though there are a few who still give out of the goodness of their hearts. A couple who breaks up, even though they are not married by law (either in church or by a Justice of the Peace), can now by law have divorces and re-marry if they choose to.

Our ancestors believed in what we call toorngaq. I do not know the specific meaning of the word; its original definition has been lost in the generations. It is obvious that a toorngaq is a spirit and not a normal human being. A human eye cannot see this being, only the shaman can see it. There are many toorngaq, which are helpers of shamans. A toorngaq can be a reincarnated human being, or it can be an animal; these are toorngaq of shamans, spirits not seen by a normal human being. When a shaman beckons these toorngaq they can be seen by that shaman. When a person gets sick, the shaman would attempt to heal that sick person through his or her powers. Sometimes those powers would work if the patient confessed all his or her sins, but if the patient refused to confess, then that patient would not be healed.

If something wrong were done in a certain community, a fear would hover over that community, and spirits would hover over that community that could not be seen by people other than the shaman. The person who committed the wrongful act would be uncovered by the shaman and the shaman would try to get that person to admit that wrongful act. If the person admitted to the wrongful act, then the joy in the community would be rekindled.

Today, with all that is going on in the world, people are not as peaceful and happy as they used to be, and sometimes even fight amongst themselves, and if they walk by each other on the road they do not even look at each other. When I first started going to the south, when I saw a person on the street I would face that person and smile, but that person would not smile back. We have become like that. We are "Eskimos" in our land.

Inuit, and not the white man or Qallunaat, should be called "Eskimo," because that refers more to the people of the Arctic and not specifically to others such as the Qallunaat.

"Inuk" can mean anything but an animal; for example, a white person, a black person, or a Japanese person can be considered as an Inuk, because that means a person.

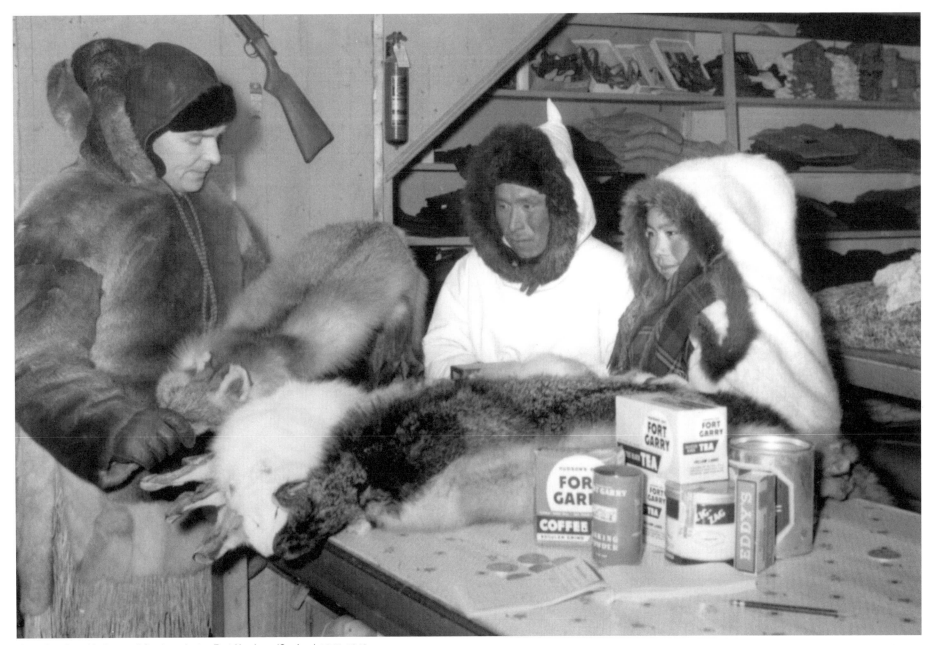

Store interior with furs and food products, Fort Harrison (Quebec) 1947–1948.

PHOTOGRAPH BY RICHARD HARRINGTON. NO DATE GIVEN — COURTESY OF THE NATIONAL ARCHIVES OF CANADA. NEG. NO. PA 129927 — RICHARD HARRINGTON COLLECTION.

OPEN LETTER TO JUSTICE J.E. RICHARD

The Honourable Mr. Justice J.E. Richard
      Jan.15.92
Supreme Court of the Northwest Territories
P.O. Box 188
Y E L L O W K N I F E / N W T   X1A 2N2

Dear Ted:

You will certainly recall our chance meeting in mid December 91 in Baker Lake/NWT. We both stayed at the Iglu Hotel, you to hold court, and I to gather material and photographs for my proposed new book, *Alaska and the Canadian North: The Voice of the Natives.*

I sat in on some of the court proceedings, both yours and Justice Bourassa's Territorial Court. His session preceded yours. You granted me the privilege to take a few photographs in the Court Room while you were addressing the jury. For that I am very grateful.

Ted, you noticed my unease about the proceedings in the Armand Tagoona case. It was obvious to me that you had a hard time reaching a verdict. You postponed your sentencing for two days after the case was heard.

He had pleaded guilty, and received a two-month jail term. Afterwards you and your entourage packed up and left Baker Lake. I observed you depart and took some photographs through the upstairs bubble window as you loaded your gear into the taxi truck. It felt kind of strange. You came, you judged, you left.

None of you good people had any obvious feeling of belonging there, or roots in the society in which you sat in judgment.

Some days later Armand Tagoona died.

Ted, you knew that I would write to you about my thoughts. We spoke about it. I choose to do so in the form of this Open Letter.

Armand Tagoona's death, totally unexpected, shook me badly. Some weeks have passed since.

Armand Tagoona is dead. But who was Armand Tagoona?

Armand Tagoona was the first Inuk to be ordained a priest. I knew about him but had not met him. An essay he wrote in Rankin Inlet in April 1991 struck me as that of a man of vision and concern for the fate of his people. He was a keen observer and good writer, fully at home in the English language. I received an English translation of his essay as well as the version in Inuktitut (a language I do not understand).

I had heard stories about Armand Tagoona from David Webster, who had been a teacher in Baker Lake for some 13 years. He had served seven years in surrounding N.W.T. settlements and consequently knew Armand Tagoona well; they were friends. Webster subsequently became the head of the Inuit Culture and Linguistics Section of Indian and Northern Affairs Canada and recently received the Order of Canada for his services to the Inuit. He was instrumental in re-introducing Inuktitut as a language of schooling in Baker Lake. He is married to an Inuk woman from that settlement.

From David I learned about Armand Tagoona's attempt to start his own church after he found Christianity wanting and incompatible with his people's experience and their all-encompassing view of life.

His new church, which he called Christian Arctic Fellowship, was intended to find a reconciliation between his people's traditional values and views, and the insufficient, strange, and foreign teachings of implanted Christianity.

But that too did not satisfy him and he came to the conclusion that all missioneering had to stop.

"If I could turn back the time, I would advise my people to send the missionaries home. And if they refuse to leave, cut their throats. We would have been better off without them."

That sentiment startled me. I longed to meet the man who had the courage to challenge the established order of such a mighty institution. Little did I know that the chance would come.

While I was in Baker Lake I met Armand Tagoona, late in the afternoon of 9 December 1991 in his home for the elderly, a short walk from the Iglu Hotel. We established and felt an instant rapport. Over a cup of coffee we talked about many things.

I was shown his published book with his own drawings, and many photographs out of his collection of albums — photographs of his father, Felix Konrad, a German-born trader for a French company; of his mother, the daughter of an Inuk woman and a white whaler of unknown origin; of his children and grandchildren. I learned a lot about his family and his life, his concerns and hopes for the future.

I showed Armand a dummy of my forthcoming book. We spoke about its text, about his essay and others. I felt that I was in the presence of a great mind, that of a vigorous and healthy man of sixty-five, only one year my senior. He was full of hope and plans for the future. We obviously shared many values.

I queried him about the part in his essay where he referred to the custom among the Inuit of having two spouses, either wives or husbands — with the full consent of all the people in the community and the families concerned. And I also asked him about his feeling toward missionaries. He confirmed the views he had earlier expressed. I asked whether he would be willing to write an essay for my book about this, and to my great delight he agreed.

He spoke quite candidly about the charges against him for sexual assault. He volunteered everything he could recall about that assault. The incident happened seven years ago. He told me how he held and cuddled a 14-year-old girl in his arms. How he touched her breast and kissed her, with her full consent. Both were fully clothed.

I had no knowledge of his pending court case. He said that he would plead guilty. According to Canadian law and also according to Christian teaching, so he said, he was guilty. Not, however, according to his conscience! He felt totally at ease with himself. And certainly he gave me the impression of being just that. "And besides," he added, "I have a good lawyer."

I took a great liking to Armand Tagoona. I asked his permission to take a couple of photographs of him. He consented. We parted, and I left for the hotel. His court appearance was slated for the next afternoon. I would be there.

Before Armand Tagoona's trial, jury selection took place in the absolutely crammed Court Room. The Canadian and Territorial flags were draped diagonally across the plastic bubble windows of the corrugated steel, half-round hotel building. Between the windows a small printed Coat of Arms was pinned to the wall to add some dignity to the otherwise utilitarian hotel banquet room in this settlement of about 1,100 inhabitants.

Two hundred people were summoned for possible jury duty. Many more women, men, and children jam-packed the overheated and stuffy room. I was an early bird, and had a front-row seat in this open court. My Leica cameras were under my chair. I wished I had been allowed to use them. But

permission was refused. Most people wore heavy clothing, parkas, boots, caps. There was simply no room to put them anywhere. Infants got fed, toddlers tried to move about between all the feet. The air got very stale, very fast. Outside the temperature was -44°C. Inside the thermometer registered +23°C. The sweat was running freely, as were the noses.

The name of every one of the two hundred jury prospects had to be called out and their presence verified. Then the selection started. For all the proceedings there was instantaneous wireless translation from English, the language of the court, to Inuktitut, the language of the natives.

Most of the elders are unilingual Inuktitut speakers. Every one of them was excused and could leave. Thereby eliminating the voice of experience! The traditional respect held for the elders' wisdom was gone as a factor in determining the fate of the accused. None of the court officials appeared to be native. Neither the crown attorney, a white woman, nor the defence counsel, indeed no white person, addressed any Inuit in their native tongue. But both crown attorney and defence counsel had an unchallengeable veto in the jury selection process.

Twelve suitable jurors were sworn in, and their hands were required to touch the Bible. I presume to ensure their honesty. I feel that to be an insult to their dignity. As if humans would otherwise be untrustworthy! That book does not have any relationship to the natives' history whatsoever. It is an instrument of enslavement and I would never swear an oath on that book.

All jurors were younger people of the community, capable of following the court proceedings in English. I did not sit in for all of the ensuing case, but I returned to hear the charges being read against Armand Tagoona later on in the day.

The accuser, a shy Inuk woman now 21 years of age, was asked by the crown attorney how she felt. In a barely audible voice and with her head bowed she replied that she felt that "God now will send me to hell." Her agony was obvious. It appeared to me that she took the teachings of Christianity, and that religion's punishing and rewarding God, quite literally.

The historical attitudes and traditions of the Inuit in sexual matters, as distinguished from those of the white man, were often certainly a question of survival. These facts seemed not to have been considered by the court at all. The mental anguish caused in this case to the young woman is, in my view, a real cause for concern, a mental crime even. The wounding of the soul of this Inuit woman by the teachings of Christianity, that religion so totally alien to all natives, is indeed tragic.

As an aside you will allow me to observe that the repercussions of this uprooting and destruction of native beliefs will be felt until the natives free themselves from it. This destruction always precedes the implantation of foreign religions and is criminal on a gigantic scale. If there were laws against mental cruelty, the entire hierarchy of all obedience- and belief-demanding, organized, missioneering religions of all stripes would sit behind bars!

Perhaps it is not surprising that your other case, also a sexual assault, ended with acquittal of the accused. That case was by judge and jury. Armand Tagoona had pleaded guilty. Before judgment day for Armand Tagoona I had a chance to interview and photograph another hamlet elder, an Inuk woman, Roda Parka. My interpreter, Sadie Hill of Ottawa, a native of Baker Lake and a niece of Roda Parka, was of course needed with her language skill to assist me.

One of my questions was in regard to the double marriage that was at times practised in the Arctic, as Armand Tagoona had described in his essay. Without the slightest surprise on her face and without even blinking an eye she simply confirmed it as accepted behaviour, although it was not practised in her family.

Two days later, on Thursday 12 December 1991, I went out for a walk in the -42 °C pre-dawn morning, a camera at the ready in my parka. The air was full of tingling ice crystals. The southeastern sky showed the first light, long before sunrise at around 10:15. An eerie atmosphere.

I had already photographed a water truck, delivering fresh water to a dwelling. A burly chap was filling the house's water tank with a big hose and a grin on his face.

My fingers were getting numb from the cold as I walked down the street, passed by the odd snowmobile or lonely pedestrian, bundled up like myself against the intense cold, now already in its unrelenting sixth day.

As chance would have it, I encountered another figure, hooded and slightly hunched against the cold. I was greeted with a warm "Good morning Hans," and realized that it was Armand Tagoona. He was walking toward the hotel to hear, later on, the Judge's verdict. There on the street, too, I took several photographs of him. I would be in the courtroom, I told him, and we went in opposite directions. He was going west, away from the light, and I, east, into it. Both of us were alone with our thoughts.

When I came back from my walk and stuffed my Leica into three different plastic bags outside the hotel to keep it from icing up inside the warm room, I found the court already in session. The verdict had not yet been read.

In the stunned silence, you, the Justice, announced a two-month prison term for Armand Tagoona, not without obvious anguish, yet with firmness, and according to the law as you interpreted it.

The defence requested and received the court's approval for the sentence to be served on weekdays only and within the local RCMP premises. Armand Tagoona's services to the community were needed over the weekends.

I sat behind Armand Tagoona and was the first to speak to him after the court was adjourned. We looked at each other, trying to read each other's mind. I was somewhat numbed. Armand seemed totally relaxed.

I left for the games room of the hotel adjoining the now defunct Court Room. That games room was full of people, many women crying. As Armand came into the room, he spoke to his people in their native Inuktitut. Even many a man took Armand by the shoulders and held him tight. It was an outpouring of affection and warmth for him.

My Leica camera remained hanging from my shoulder. I felt like an intruder, unwilling to disturb. In hindsight I regret not having photographed what I saw — a healthy-looking and outwardly calm man, seemingly at ease with himself.

Some days later Armand Tagoona was dead. The stated cause: internal bleeding. I wonder!

Ted, the natives' inherent right to self-government, to their own justice system, to their own beliefs and values, has always been theirs. It evolved over many, many generations of living in one of the harshest climates on earth. They existed and thrived in their own way, without us white people. They do not have to plead or negotiate for this!

We white people have never had the right to take these fundamental rights away from them Consequently you have no moral or even legal right to sit in judgment on any aspects of their lives; nor has any other white judge. Human dignity demands that!

Natives everywhere would have evolved at their own pace, and will again. They are now "re-greening." Their roots take nourishment again from their own soil. Their pride will come back, and with it their dignity and self-esteem, now almost totally destroyed.

We, the intruders, have upset their equilibrium, caused them physical, and, even worse, mental harm. We had better face that reality. We have made them dependent on us and our welfare handouts. That system has to be disbanded — not with shock treatment, but at the natives' bidding.

We have become interdependent, but we have to let go of the strings we forceably attached to them.

Listen to the natives, and listen closely! We will all benefit!

Ted, I am glad our paths have crossed!

With personal regards
Hans-Ludwig Blohm

P.S. After my return from the north I met with Iain Baines of Canada Post. I had worked with him on a variety of projects. He asked me what I was up to these days. I told him about my trip to Baker Lake, about Armand Tagoona, about his court case. That meeting was before I learned about Armand Tagoona's death. He asked me if I had seen the set of four stamps about Canadian Folk Tales that had been published on 1 October 1991.

Published at the same time was a book with illustrations about these four legends and a short form of the written legends themselves.

Inuit in office, Port Harrison (Quebec) 1947–1948.

PHOTOGRAPH BY RICHARD HARRINGTON — COURTESY OF THE NATIONAL ARCHIVES OF CANADA. NEG. NO. PA 129928 — RICHARD HARRINGTON COLLECTION.

Iain Baines was the coordinator for this project. I knew and had used the stamps, but I had not seen the booklet.

One of the legends, "Kaujjakjuk," is from the eastern Arctic. Deborah Evaluatjuk, a totally bilingual native from Igloolik, had adapted this still very much alive legend for this booklet.

Ted, get a copy of this booklet. It is a must! It is a story about an orphan boy who got badly mistreated and finally seeks revenge. In the end both he, the orphan, and his shaman brother married two Inuk women each. Baines told me that Canada Post has never received so many negative comments about anything they ever published. Read and think about it.

I learned in a very short time from three different sources about the Inuit history of double-spousing, for lack of a better word. And we dare sit in judgment about their behaviour. Whether you or I like it or abhor it is totally irrelevant. But the historical lifestyles of the Inuit or any other natives is certainly very relevant to them. We'd better get out of their hair, as fast as is reasonably possible!

After my return from another trip to the Arctic from April to June 1992, I found the following reply from Justice Richard, handwritten on Supreme Court stationery. [see page 153]

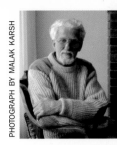

PHOTOGRAPH BY MALAK KARSH

INTRODUCTION TO
HANS-LUDWIG BLOHM

My photographs for: *The Voice of the Natives: The Canadian North and Alaska* came about over a long period of time, in the vastness of the North, it's diverse geographical regions and climates. The challenge of the various seasons never deterred me from actively trying to capture its spirit. If that is at all possible — photographically.

Integral to that spirit are the people.

It is the soul of its people that allows you, consciously or sub-consciously, to recognize, feel, and experience this spirit. It expresses itself in their faces — at many levels.

If some of what moved me, as a human being, comes across to you as viewer, you too might feel *The Voice of the Natives: The Canadian North and Alaska* as I felt and heard it, in my heart and soul. **HB**

— Hans-Ludwig Blohm

II, III

VIII, IX

HANS-LUDWIG BLOHM

X, XI

XII, XIII

XIV, XV, XVI

XVII, XVIII

XIX, XXI, XX

XXII, XXIII, XXIV, XXV

HANS-LUDWIG BLOHM

XLII, XLIII

XLIV, XLV

XLVI, XLVII

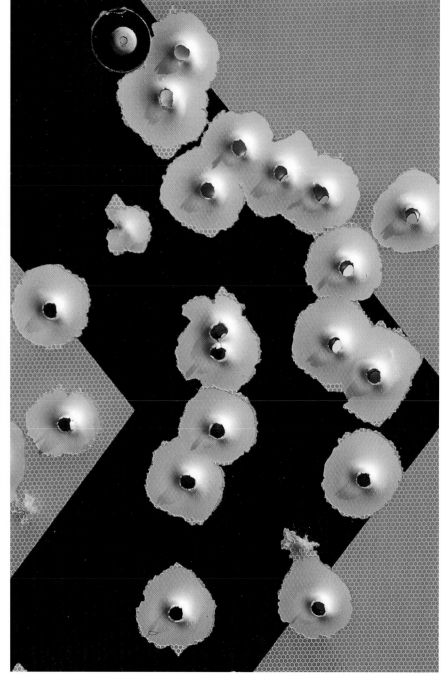

HANS-LUDWIG BLOHM

83

HANS LUDWIG BLOHM '85

LIV, LV, LVI

LVII, LVIII

LIX, LX

LXIX, LXX

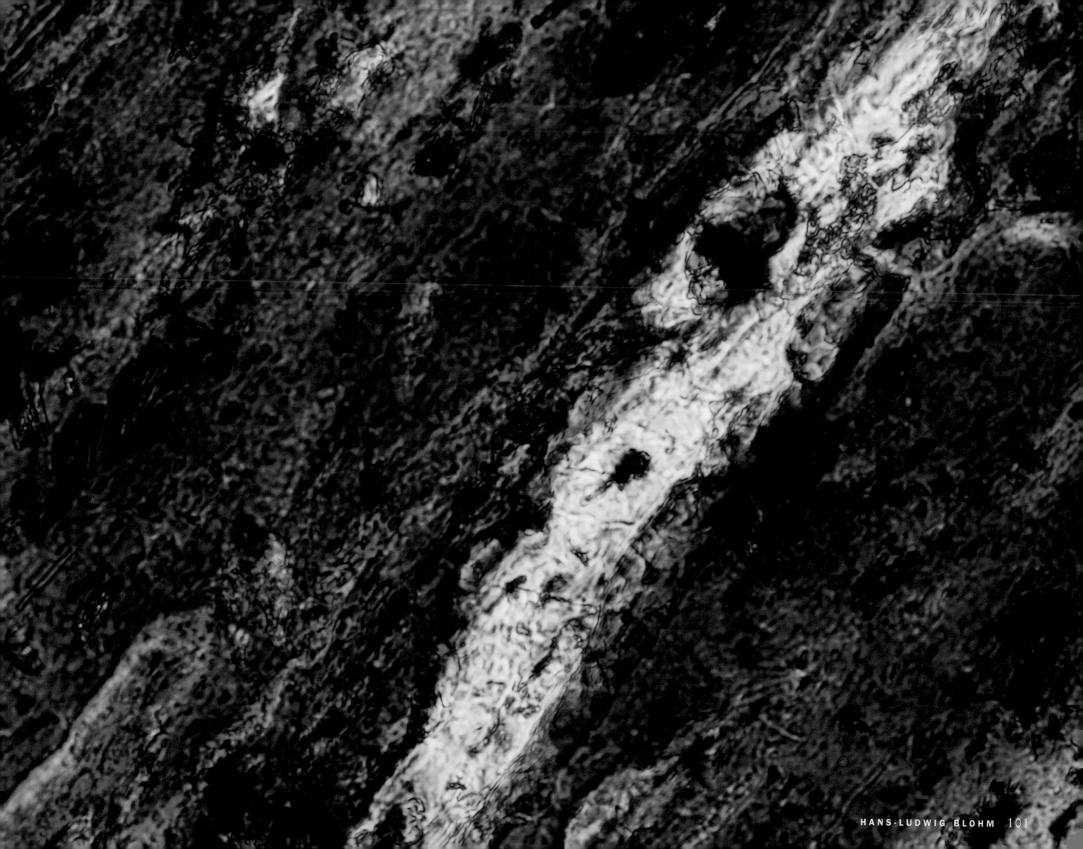

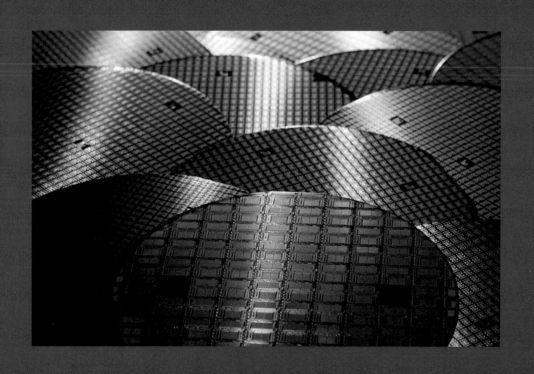

LXXVIII, LXXIX, LXXX

LXXXI, LXXXII

LXXXIII, LXXXIV

LXXXV, LXXXVI

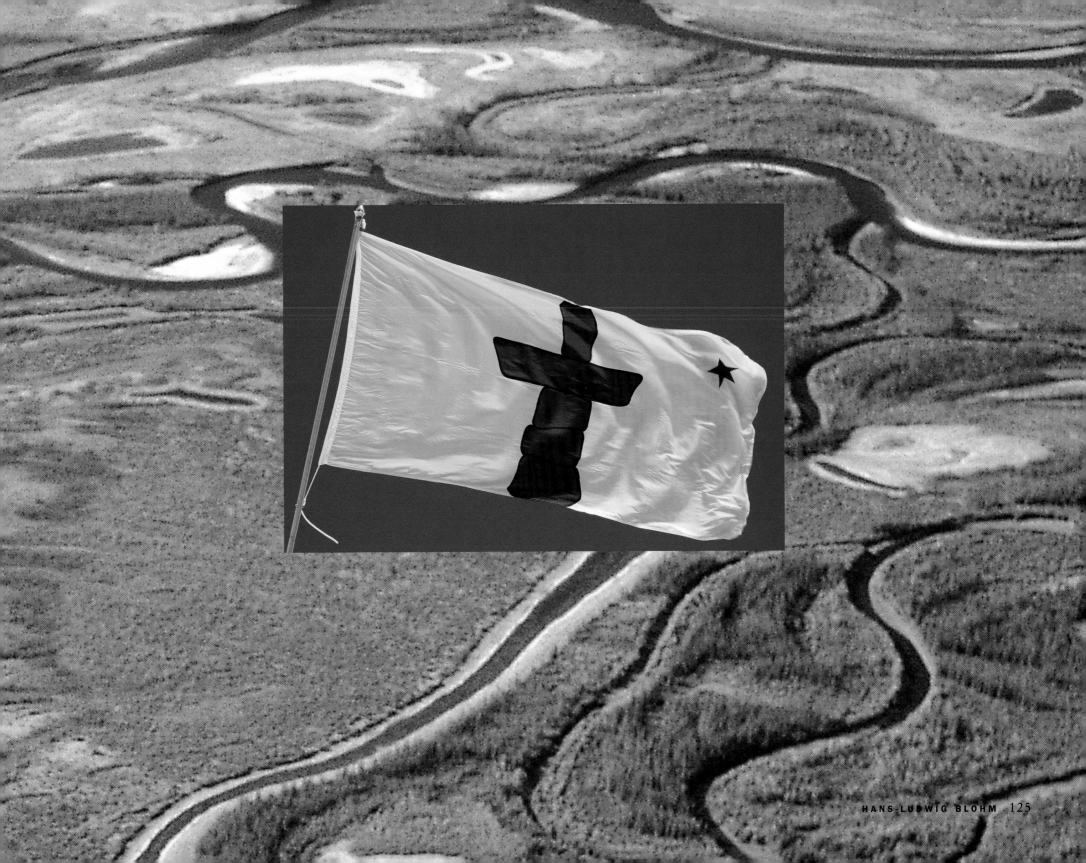

CV, CVI, CVII, CVIII

HANS·LUDWIG BLOHM 135

CIX, CX

CXIV, CXV

CXVIII, CXIX

CXX, CXXI

HANS-LUDWIG BLOHM

Songs are like thoughts, brought forward with your breath when human beings are moved with great power, events and spirits, that common words can no longer express.

These words, translated here by me from German and certainly by some body else from the original native language, are attributed to:

– *Opingalik*, a Netsilik Eskimo

PHOTO ESSAY —
THE VOICE OF THE NATIVES

I   Rosemarie Kuptana: former President, Inuit Tapirisat of Canada.

II   Drum dance: festivities in large Igloo during signing of Nunavut Land Claims Agreement in principle. Igloolik, May 1990.

III   Drum dance: proclaiming the new Canadian Territory of Nunavut. Iqaluit, April 1999.

IV   Barnabas Pirjuaq: respected elder in his home. Baker Lake, December 1991.

V   Emma Feichtinger: respected elder. Tuktuyaktuk, April 1992.

VI   Zebedee Nungak: in traditional kayak with Arctic char tied to the deck. Kangirsuk, Nunavik (a.k.a. Arctic Quebec), August 1994.

VII   Paul Utatnaarq: elder with his dogteam on the ice. Baker Lake, December 1991.

VIII   Inukshuk: Inuit landmark. Rankin Inlet, Nunavut.

IX   Two mountains in ice fog. Ogilvie Mountains, Yukon.

X   Ice Crystal. Yukon.

XI   Floating ice. Pond Inlet, Baffin Island, Nunavut.

XII   Polar bear and caribou. Labrador.

XIII   Polar bear. Ramah Bay, Atlantic coast of Labrador.

XIV   Coastal Island. Atlantic coast of Labrador.

XV   *SS Manakoora*: Nachvak fiord. Torngat Mountains, Labrador.

XVI   *SS Manakoora*: fog and icebergs approaching the abandoned settlement of Hebron (Moravian Mission Station and Hudson Bay trading post), Labrador.

XVII   First Nations: march and rally in front of the Peace Tower of Parliament Hill. Ottawa, July 1992.

XVIII   First Nations teepee encampment at Le Breton Flats. Ottawa, June 1993.

XIX   Hyacinthe Andre: former band chief, Gwich'in Indian Settlement. Arctic Red River, Northwest Territories.

XX   Christy Thompson: Gwich'in Indian elder from Aklavik, NWT, during the Gwich'in land claim settlement festivities. Ft. McPherson, Northwest Territories, April 1992.

XXI   Margaret Thompson: Tetlit Gwich'in Council in Ft. McPherson, Northwest Territories, holding portrait print of her mother outside Band Council Building, April 1999.

XXII   Traditional house and pole detail. K'san village, northern British Columbia, 1999.

XXIII   Haida Burial Totem. Anthony Island, Queen Charlotte Islands, British Columbia, 1980.

XXIV   Totem Pole. Kitwanga, northern British Columbia.

XXV   Native boy climbing totem pole. Kitwanga, northern British Columbia, 1979.

XXVI   Jimbob and Bradley Firth: Gwich'n Indian trappers with furs at their cabin. Ft. McPherson, Northwest Territories, April 1992.

XXVII   Ancient and modern transportation: awaiting transfer of then Federal Minister of Indian and Northern Affairs, Tom Siddon, from jet to sled, for the signing of the Tetlin Gwich'in land claim settlement. Ft. McPherson, April 1992.

XXVIII   Ft. Hope Drummers: during the Tetlin Gwich'in land claim settlement festivities. Ft. McPherson, Northwest Territories, April 1992.

XXIX   Inuvialuit "Delta Drum Dancers" of Inuvik, Northwest Territories, during the "Royal Assent" festivities for the land claim settlement to establish Nunavut. Coppermine, Nunavut, July 1993.

XXX   Youngsters on playground. Iqaluit, Nunavut, April 1990.

XXXI   Youngsters at play on dock. Nain, Labrador, 1993.

XXXII–   Four images taken during tenth Annual Meeting of
XXXV   "Pauktutit," the Inuit Women's Institute. Iqaluit, Nunavut, February 1994.

XXXVI   Susan Avinga: tending seal oil lamp in ceremonial Igloo during festivities for the signing of the Nunavut Land Claim Agreement in principle. Igloolik, Northwest Territories, May 1990.

XXXVII   Mother and child in Igloo. Igloolik, Northwest Territories, May 1990.

XXXVIII   Two boys on bicycles during a blizzard. Igloolik, Northwest Territories, May 1990.

XXXIX   Youngster and dog playing below Canadian flag during blizzard. Igloolik, Northwest Territories, May 1990.

XL   Elisabeth Avinga. Igloolik, Northwest Territories, May 1990.

XLI   Co-op. Coffee shop during blizzard. Igloolik, Northwest Territories, May 1990.

XLII   Lynx in leghold trap along trapline crossing the Canol Road. Yukon, April 1982.

XLIII   Arctic hare feeding on arctic willow. Anaktuvuk Pass, Alaska.

XLIV   Catching the last rays of sunlight. Ogilvie Mountains, Yukon, in mid-January.

XLV   January winter twilight in the Yukon.

XLVI   Migrating swan on small, half-frozen lake. Alaska, May 1999.

XLVII   Migrating swans and ducks during snowfall on small pond. Alaska.

XLVIII   Welcoming sign along Alaska Highway. Alaska.

XLIX   Welcome to Alaska! Shot up highway sign, common throughout the State.

L   Alaska State flag.

LI   Mount Mckinley: seen from Talkeetna, early morning in late April.

LII   Mount McKinley: 20,320 feet. Denali National Park, Alaska, 2:30 A.M. in July.

LIII   Caribou herd. Anaktuvuk Pass, Brooks Range, Alaska.

LIV   Russian Orhodox church. Kenai, Alaska.

LV   Ripe "Alaska size" blueberries.

LVI   Inupiat elders meeting. Kotzebue, Alaska, May 1992.

LVII   Town of Kodiak. Kodiak Island, Alaska.

LVIII   Fishplant workers: cleaning a fresh catch of black cod. Sitka, Alaska.

LIX   A spring evening in Alaska's largest city. Anchorage, 1999.

LX   Getting ready for take-off at floatplane base. Anchorage, Alaska.

LXI   Fairbanks-based Frontier Flying Service Inc.'s German-built Dornier twin turbojet approaching the settlement of Kaktovik, Alaska, on Barter Island in the frozen Beaufort Sea, May.

LXII   A modern First Air jet unloading passengers and cargo at Canada's most northern scheduled airport. Resolute Bay, Nunavut, October 2000.

LXIII   A small plane makes a less than successful landing on emergency airstrip along the still unfinished Yukon section of the Dempster Highway, summer 1977.

LXIV   Glare ice. Alaska Highway.

LXV   Placer Miner Peter Ericson: a handful of gold at the abandoned Hunker Creek mine. Dawson City area, Yukon, 1979.

LXVI Alaska's "liquid gold" flowing through the Alaska pipeline in the foothills of the Brooks Range, transporting raw oil from Prudhoe Bay on the Beaufort Sea to the terminal in Valdez on the Prince William Sound of the northern Pacific.

LXVII Harbour and settlement during the peak of oil exploration activities. Tuktoyaktuk, Northwest Territories, 1980.

LXVIII At ground level. Tuktoyaktuk, 1992.

LXIX The Barren lands of Nunavut with hundreds of thousands of bodies of water, seen from a small plane during the short arctic summer month.

LXX A highly magnified thin section of mineral-bearing rock under polarized light and a gypsum red # 1 filter.

LXXI Satellite receiving dish during the twilight hours. Baker Lake, Nunavut, December 1991.

LXXII Modern communication links in the north are extensive. Silicone chips as seen on the "wafers" here, are the miniscule but vital building blocks that link all northern communities via satellite.

LXXIII Large open pit and fully operational Ekati Diamond mine, several hundred kilometres north of Yellowknife. December 2000.

LXXIV Raw diamonds from Toronto-based Twin Mine Corp.'s exploration site near Kangiqsualujjuaq, Nunavik's Ungava Bay's east coast.

LXXV Harsh light. Tombstone Valley, Ogilvie Mountains, Yukon.

LXXVI– Bald Eagle. Homer, Kenai Peninsula, Alaska,
LXXVII Spring 1999.

LXXVIII Arctic Cotton Grass. Nunavik.

LXXIX Arctic Poppies. Nunavik.

LXXX Arctic Wildflowers. Nunavik.

LXXXI Took River. Alaska Range, Alaska.

LXXXII Autumn in the Foothills. Wrangell Mountains, Alaska.

LXXXIII Setting sun. Queen Charlotte Islands.

LXXXIV Heavy weather. Pacific coast straddling Alaska and northern British Columbia.

LXXXV Hoary Marmot.

LXXXVI Purple Saxifrage.

LXXXVII Jimmy Carpenter and Roy Lengenberg: Inuit soapstone carvers at the entrance of their small carving shed. Coppermine, Nunavut, Summer 1993.

LXXXVIII Gerry Kigiuna with his soapstone sculpture of an Inuk in a hunting kayak. Coppermine, Nunavut, Summer 1993.

LXXXIX Nunavut: the largest ever Canadian-made stone print, presented by the artist Kenojuak at the signing ceremony for the Nunavut Land Claim Agreement. Iqaluit, Nunavut, May 1993. Only three prints have been drawn of this highly acclaimed work of art.

XC Kenojuak Ashevak, the famous artist from Cape Dorset, Baffin Island, Nunavut, on the day she presented her stone print to the large gathering assembled for the signing of the Nunavut Land Claim Agreement. Iqaluit, May 1993.

XCI Celebration and feast after the signing of the

XCII Nunavut Land Claim Agreement in principle. Igloolik, May 1990.

XCIII Young people proudly show their new settlement and regional flags after royal assent was given for the establishment of Nunanvut. Coppermine, July 1993.

XCIV An unknown, but very proud young girl showing her allegiance to Nunavut as part of Canada. Iqaluit, May 1993.

XCV Nunavut has "arrived": Coca-Cola distribution truck. Iqaluit, Nunavut.

XCVI Nunavut flag, first shown in Iqaluit, Nunavut, April 1999.

XCVII Jose Kusugak: former President of Nunavut Tungavik Inc., addressing dignitaries and audience during the inauguration of Nunavut. Iqaluit, April 1999.

XCVIII Mary Simon-May: Canada's first Ambassador for Circumpolar Affairs, addressing the Royal Commission on aboriginal peoples hearing. Ottawa, 1993,

XCIX Three kids on street. Umiujaq, Nunavik, August 1984.

C Youngsters with remote control toys on the Hudson Bay shore. Umiujaq, Nunavik, August 1994.

CI Inuit mother and child in amautik. Coppermine, Nunavut, July 1993.

CII Safe and warm in modern housing: Thomashaw Augiak with grandchildren. Kangirsuk, Nunavik, January 1992.

CIII Honourable J.E. (Ted) Richard: Senior Judge of the Supreme Court of the Northwest Territories, addressing a jury during Court proceedings. Baker Lake, Nunavut, December 1991.

CIV Armand Tagoona: in the early morning hours of a bitter cold December day (- 44 ˚C) on the way to his trial by judge only. Baker Lake, Nunavut, December 1991.

CV A human figure under a blanket in a solitary confinement cell photographed through a one-way window, Baffin Correctional Centre. Iqaluit, Nunavut, January 1993.

CVI Dormitory and inmates at the Baffin Correctional Centre. Iqaluit, Nunavut, January 1993.

CVII An Inuk grave. Saklet Fiord, Labrador, August 1993.

CVIII A modern Native grave. Puvirnituq, Nunavik, January 1992.

CIX Thule Eskimo house of whalebones. Resolute Bay, Nunavut, September 2000.

CX Resolute Bay, Nunavut, September 2000.

CXI– First Inuit Fashion Show during the tenth Annual
CXIII Meeting of "Pauktutit" (Inuit Women's Institute), Iqaluit, Nunavut, February 1994.

CXIV Young Inuit parents with baby, bottle-fed by father. Igloolik, Nunavut, May 1990.

CXV Four Generations of the Flaherty Family. Iqaluit, Nunavut, February 1994.

CXVI Learning lost snow skills. Puvirnituq, Nunavik, Winter 1992.

CXVII Cheerful youngsters. Puvirnituq, Nunavik, August 1994.

CVXVIII Mackenzie River Delta.

CXIX Slave River Delta.

CXX Rainbow. Richardson Mountains, Yukon, Northwest Territories.

CXXI Northern lights. Yellowknife, Northwest Territories, December 2000.

CXXII Raven in flight: Yellowknife, Northwest Territories, December 2000.

CXXIII Midnight sun. Bathurst Inlet, Nunavut, 00:05 A.M., July 2001.

TABLE OF OLD AND NEW PLACE NAMES

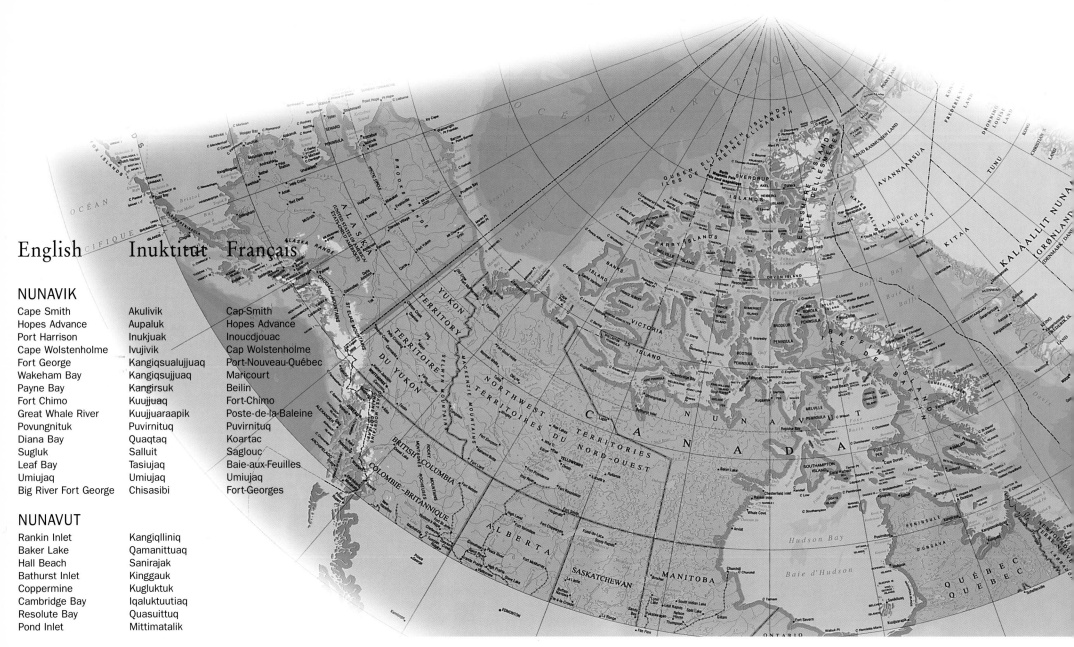

English   Inuktitut   Français

NUNAVIK

English	Inuktitut	Français
Cape Smith	Akulivik	Cap-Smith
Hopes Advance	Aupaluk	Hopes Advance
Port Harrison	Inukjuak	Inoucdjouac
Cape Wolstenholme	Ivujivik	Cap Wolstenholme
Fort George	Kangiqsualujjuaq	Port-Nouveau-Québec
Wakeham Bay	Kangiqsujjuaq	Maricourt
Payne Bay	Kangirsuk	Beilin
Fort Chimo	Kuujjuaq	Fort-Chimo
Great Whale River	Kuujjuaraapik	Poste-de-la-Baleine
Povungnituk	Puvirnituq	Puvirnituq
Diana Bay	Quaqtaq	Koartac
Sugluk	Salluit	Saglouc
Leaf Bay	Tasiujaq	Baie-aux-Feuilles
Umiujaq	Umiujaq	Umiujaq
Big River Fort George	Chisasibi	Fort-Georges

NUNAVUT

English	Inuktitut
Rankin Inlet	Kangiqlliniq
Baker Lake	Qamanittuaq
Hall Beach	Sanirajak
Bathurst Inlet	Kinggauk
Coppermine	Kugluktuk
Cambridge Bay	Iqaluktuutiaq
Resolute Bay	Quasuittuq
Pond Inlet	Mittimatalik

NORTHWEST TERRITORIES

English	Inuktitut
Arctic Red River	Tsiigetchie

MAP COURTESY OF: ENERGY, MINES, AND RESOURCE

A LETTER TO HANS-L BLOHM

The Honourable Mr. Justice J.E. Richard

1 May 1992

Dear Hans

Your welcome letter ended up in a pile of unread correspondence and articles beside my desk. It is only today, after many weeks of circuits and absences from my office that I have taken the time to sit down and read your letter and enclosures.

Thank you very much for the slides, the Tagoona essay, and the copy of the Kaujjakjuk legend.

Also, Hans, I do appreciate you sharing your thoughts with me, following your observation in the Courtroom. Privately, I agree with much of what you say. Although I have heard many of these things expressed before, I am grateful to have an "outsider" (lay person) share his thoughts about our justice system, in the context of personal observation of a specific case.

I am not one who will stand in the way of "community justice" for our aboriginal peoples. It is a solution — but it must come from the community people themselves, and not from us.

I, too, am glad that our paths have crossed, & perhaps one day we will meet again, when we will hopefully have more time to converse.

Regards
Ted

THE HONOURABLE MR. JUSTICE J.E. RICHARD

JUDGE'S CHAMBERS
P.O. BOX 188
YELLOWKNIFE, N.W.T.
X1A 2N2

May 1/92

Dear Hans

Your welcome letter ended up in a pile of unread correspondence and articles beside my desk. It is only today, after many weeks of circuits and absences from my office that I have taken the time to sit down & read your letter & enclosures.

Thank you very much for the slides, the Tagoona essay, and the copy of the Kaujjakjuk legend.

Also, Hans, I do appreciate you sharing your thoughts with me, following your observations in the Courtroom. Privately, I agree with much of what you say. Although I have heard many of these things expressed before, I am grateful to have an "outsider" (lay person) share his thoughts about our justice system, in the context of personal observation of a specific case.

I am not one who will stand in the way of "community justice" for our aboriginal peoples. It is a solution — but it must come from the community people themselves, and not from us.

I, too, am glad that our paths crossed, & perhaps one day we will meet again, when we hopefully will have more time to converse.

Regards
Ted

INTRODUCTION TO BARNABAS PIRJUAQ

While in Baker Lake I interviewed Barnabas Pirjuaq, a respected elder, aged 66, a man who has been changed from a nomadic hunter used to living in igloos and tents while roaming the country in search of food and shelter, to a hamlet-dweller in a two-storey well-insulated house with an oil furnace, hot and cold running water, and flush toilets.

From legends and story-telling, singing and games, to multi-channel TV and video. From subsistence-living with all its uncertainties, triumphs, and satisfactions, to a cash society with welfare handouts from the Qallunaat. From independence to almost total dependence. No other generation has had to bridge such a tremendous gap in a single lifetime. Only if one knows the Arctic can one imagine the strength required to adapt to such rapid change — and survive.

My questions in English were translated by Barnabas's niece, Sadie Hill of Ottawa. The interview was recorded on tape and subsequently transcribed by Sadie Hill. **HB**

BEFORE THE QALLUNAAT CAME

Barnabas Pirjuaq

Blohm

Now, if you would talk about what life was like before Qallunaat came, especially of men's and women's responsibilities.

Pirjuaq

This year, 1991, I am 66 years of age. I am very knowledgeable on the subject of survival today and before the Qallunaat came. I have other concerns regarding income, especially now, because money is needed to survive today. Before more Qallunaat came to settle in Baker Lake I remember that there were only five: two RCMP officers, one Roman Catholic priest, one Hudson's Bay Company clerk, and one Anglican minister; these people were the only Qallunaat at the time.

In those times, the young couple who were married were taught their responsibilities, and if food and skins for clothing weren't scarce, survival did not seem hard, because we did not know any way of life other than that.

As children got a little older, the parents who were very good hunters or good tailors could not teach their own children. Other parents taught them and their own; if a child was a boy he was taught by his father, though he was not always aware that he was learning, because he enjoyed thinking he was just going along on a hunting trip. He learned how to hunt and make an igloo by watching and trying to help (as children will always want to do the things that anyone is doing). The father did not directly tell his son that he was going to teach him how to hunt

or trap, but took him along on his winter and summer trips so he could learn by watching. By the time the child reaches seven or eight years of age he has learned quite a lot, but children who are four or five years old are still too young.

If the child was a little girl she was taught by her mother how to sew, prepare skins, and cook meals. It was just like going to school every morning; they learned all of these things from their parents.

When boys were going to learn to use a rifle, they did not start off by shooting caribou, they were first taught using a 22-calibre rifle to hunt ptarmigans. And though you can get very close to a ptarmigan, they are very small targets, so when a boy has learned to aim at a ptarmigan, it becomes obvious that he can hunt caribou.

Same with teaching girls: they did not learn how to make qulittaq (caribou parkas) right at the start. They first learned how to make mittens and kamiks (caribou boots), to soften the skins.

Before the Qallunaat came, our forefathers taught their children in a sensible logical way — a boy child so that he can be the stronger one, the one who can handle being outdoors, has to be taught about those things, to be able to hunt on his own. As for the girl child, because she gets cold quicker and is weaker she has to be taught about things that need doing indoors. Because the female gets cold quicker and is weaker than the male, she was taught how to do things that she'll need to know about making clothes and cooking. In those days the parents who were getting a daughter-in-law watched that they would get one who was already knowledgeable about sewing and preparing food, or a son-in-law who already knew how to hunt, one who was already taught by the mother if she was a girl and one who was taught by his father if he were a boy, even if they lived in different camps. What Inuit were taught made a lot of sense, the only difference being that the children were taught by the father or older brother. And if they were orphans they would be taught by their uncles. That makes sense, we know that the males are and always have been the stronger, they were taught to have good sense and the parents knew what they should be taught.

If the parents had a number of sons and they married, they tested their daughters-in-law (two or three) about what they were more talented at. If a daughter-in-law was good at sewing on her own she was treated not as a servant, but someone to envy. She would not be asked to cook, fetch water, or gather firewood. There were even times when the younger ones thought the daughter-in-law was a favourite, but she was treated a certain way because of her abilities. All daughters-in-law were tested by the parents. Only the mother would test her new daughter-in-law to find out her abilities; the father did not interfere or talk to the girl to help her. Her sewing skills would be tested, but if she were the type who did not like to just sit around indoors, she would be the one who did chores outdoors, like fetching water or gathering firewood. It was as if they were treated like servants to fetch things, but it was not because they weren't loved. Her responsibilities would depend on what she likes to do, what she had a talent for.

Inuit parents have always made sure that their children were well prepared to take on responsibilities on their own, because once the mother was gone they had to make their own clothing. And if the father died, then the eldest brother would become the head of the family. It's like the manager at the Hudson's Bay store: he has quite a number of employees; it is up to him what their jobs are, depending on their abilities. That was how the children were taught, depending on their talents and abilities.

Even though now it is much easier to get things, and money is easy to get, it is very important that the girls know how to sew, because the Inuit land will always have winters, and winters will always be very cold. Before the Qallunaat came, children were also taught by being made to do things on their own. Today even women go hunting, because now ski-doos and canoes make things easier, whereas long ago women were not given a choice; they had to stay home. That is one of the things that has changed in our way of life. There will always be winters here and they will always be harsh, even if the women stop learning how to sew. One of the important things to learn is how to prepare caribou skins, and I was going to show you these two caribou leg skins; one of them is prepared, the other isn't. When they haven't been prepared, they don't look like they are good for anything useful. To prepare the skins, they are chewed to make them more supple so they do not tear at their first use. Scrapers soften them and then a sakuut (an instrument to soften the skin more). These are kinds of things that still need to be learned today. I have a pair of mittens that white people say are very warm, but if I wore them outdoors all day and they got animal blood on them or they got wet, they would freeze, and the only thing to do would be to dry them before wearing them again. If these mitts made from caribou skin got wet or got animal blood on them, they could be cleaned, even outdoors, by rubbing them in snow and beating the snow off again with a stick. But these made from man-made material cannot be cleaned in the same way, they would just tear. Caribou skin does not get wrecked in cold weather. Weather here will always be harsh, as it always has been, so knowing how to sew clothing is still very important.

As I was saying before, some people would be treated like they were slaves at times; even I don't want to go back to that way of life. I don't want to have to get firewood of lichen and willow, because they burn much too quickly, especially in the inland area, where Inuit live away from the coast where there aren't any seals for the oil that the coastal Inuit use for cooking. Lichens and willows for firewood can be very difficult to come by even if you walk a great distance. We used lichen and willows for firewood to cook before Qallunaat came and it was one of the hard things we had to go through, especially when winter came. It isn't that important if the young people do not learn about looking for firewood, because it is not needed now, as it used to be. It is still very important to learn how to make caribou skin clothing and hunting, because they will always be used. Even though there are still elder women who have the knowledge to make caribou skin clothing, some Inuit have started going hunting without warm skin clothes. Here in our home we have always preserved caribou skins that are to be made for clothing, kamiks, and mittens for winter. Because clothing will always be important, we want our children to know how to prepare skins and sew them. Anyone can learn how to prepare skins for sewing. Inuit always made different sizes of clothing, depending on what size the person wore, because Inuit have always been different sizes, so their clothing would always be made to fit properly.

Women always knew how to make clothing. Men would help with softening the caribou skins if the weather was not good for hunting, but not when it came to cutting the patterns for clothing.

I did not even learn how to make mitts. Though I know how to soften skins.

It will always be useful and important for women to be able to make caribou skin clothing, the same way a man has to learn to be a guide. Qallunaat, when they come up north, have never asked a woman to be their guide. A man has to learn about travelling, even if he is not going hunting. Here the wind always comes from the north, so that the snowdrifts are formed by the north wind. For this reason men, even young men, should learn about the formation of the snowdrifts so that even if it gets dark or if it is not a clear day, a man can still reach his destination, even if it is a long way off, without getting lost. During the winter season especially, using snowdrift formations is always as good as a compass for not getting lost. Today I use a compass too, when I never used to before they were introduced.

Blohm

How did you learn about using snow and other aids to find the direction you want to travel?

Pirjuaq

People should always look for indicators out on the land while travelling so they do not end up getting lost if the weather got bad or it gets hard to see, because you can always still see the ground you are on. For instance, if he had to go south what he would do is check out the land first, just like he would use a compass, so he knows in what direction he should be heading.

Another thing that a man must learn how to do is how to make an igloo, so that when he acts as a guide for tourists he will be considered a very good one. It is necessary to know how to do that because if the tourist from the south gets someone who just knows

how to travel and not how to construct an igloo, he will get very cold during the trip. Not all types of snow are good for making an igloo. So a man has to know what type of snow to look for when he is going to make one. In the old days, all men used to travel and make igloos along the way. But that isn't the way now; not everyone knows anymore.

Here in Baker Lake, if someone from the south comes for a holiday and asks an Inuk to take him out on the land, we try to accommodate him with someone who's knowledgeable in making an igloo quickly, or one we are sure will not get lost with him, because accidents like those can happen anytime. The only way a man can learn how to make an igloo is by becoming knowledgeable on what type of snow is better for an igloo.

So it is very important that a man knows his way around on the land and how to make an igloo. It is the same with a woman being able to make caribou skin clothing. I am saying this because if you were a guide on a trip to Gjoa Haven, for example, you could lose the opportunity to make money if you do not know how to make an igloo or know your way around on the land.

Today we use money more than we did, to live on. Before that we did not use money too much to buy food, after the Hudson's Bay Company came. It was in 1958 that we Inuit started seeing large amounts of money, when the federal government workers started giving out welfare money to buy food. That was the beginning of Inuit using money to buy what they need.

Blohm

How did the Inuit way of life start to change after the white man came?

Pirjuaq

Life started changing quite a lot in 1958. There weren't any schools built before that year. The first school that was built was smaller than the house we're living in now, and it was shared by both the older and youngest schoolchildren. And ever since that year women did not sew as much and men did not make igloos as much anymore.

Blohm

Were the children pulled away from the outpost camps to attend school, or were parents made to move to the settlements so their children could attend school?

Pirjuaq

Even though their children were attending school in the settlement, the federal government settlement managers told some parents they could go back to the land if they wanted to. But the education department told the Inuit that the children had to attend school. So some children would be picked up by plane to attend during the school year. I think I remember correctly when I say that you and your brother [Barnabas is now directly speaking to his niece Sadie Hill] were picked up to go back to Baker Lake to attend school, leaving your parents behind living at Schultz Lake.

Because children and parents did not like having to live away from each other and parents wanted their children to attend school, the number of people in the settlement started to grow. Inuit do not oppose education. As families moved into the settlement, the government got concerned about the Inuit living out on the land. They preferred to have everyone in one community in case there was starvation, and because otherwise some children wouldn't see or hear from their families for the whole summer.

That was how the Inuit gathered to live in the settlement of Baker Lake.

The difference from how it was then is that today even the younger Inuit can collect welfare, if they do not have jobs. During 1959 and even 1960, people who were not elderly or were not in bad health did not receive welfare. Things don't happen overnight. It all takes time for things to get straightened out.

Something else new is that even when the parents are working, young people can apply for welfare when they turn 18, even if they still live at their parents' home. It's easier now to receive welfare assistance.

And though these things are here to make life easier, men still need to know how to travel out on the land, how to make an igloo, and women still need to know how to make caribou skin clothing. Those are two of the things of the Inuit culture that we have to hold on to.

The way our life used to be is that some Inuit would run out of food and be without for the whole winter, because the caribou herd had already passed through. So then a relative or someone else would make sure that his family and dogs had enough to eat, but with no need to worry about actually paying it back. The person had helped the other in time of need, and did not really expect anything back, but would be helped later on in turn, if hardship came his way. That is how Inuit looked out for each other before the white people came. Some men do catch more caribou than others, if they live where there is more wildlife, while some others do not. So they took turns to help each other out. It was like having your own social services that we have today. Today when Inuit young people catch wildlife they take their catch home directly, instead of taking it to their parents. Our own children have not started doing that yet. They still bring their catch home to us

because they know we will take care of what needs to be done, cutting it up to cooking size or making dried meat. This new way of life that Inuit live now, with young people taking their catch home instead of to their parents, is not good. The wildlife officers admonish people for doing that, because caribou meat is just thrown out to the garbage by the young when the meat starts to go bad, and left outside during the spring thaw. This too has to be re-established within the Inuit way of life, to leave their wildlife catch with their parents, because hunting is very much part of our way of life. If the meat were left with the parents, you would never see it just thrown out in the garbage.

It used to be very important for families to stay together, to help each other, to support each other. I used to have two older stepbrothers, Ukpagaq and Amitnaaq, and I would go trapping with them. Then later, when we went to a trading post, I would not bother buying anything for myself, because I knew that they would get me what I needed at that time. We used dog teams for travelling. The older ones in Inuit families used to be the ones who were responsible for the other members of their household. But today, money is managed very differently. The person who gets a cheque now gets to keep the money himself. We used fox pelts as money in those days and the older ones would be the ones who chose for us what we needed. The man of the household or the eldest son kept an eye out for what the son or younger brother needed, and the younger ones were happy when they were bought some things they needed. That is as it was then. Another thing that has always been part of our way of life is that the youngest child never had the responsibility of taking care of the others in case they might need something. But the eldest child, because he grew up seeing his siblings grow up, will

never stop caring for his younger siblings or his own sons. Even I, though I did not make purchases, would always give my catch to our elders, because my dogs would be fed as well. This is part of Inuit culture, the way we thought then.

In those days Inuit did not live in one community, with a mayor. We travelled to where there was wildlife, and the children always knew it would be up to the father to manage the household and decide where they would go. He would be the one who decides where they would camp, where hunting would be good. He would tell his family, "This area may not have caribou now, but come spring there will be plenty." And it would turn out to be true. So then they would dry caribou meat that summer and when the season came to cache caribou meat they would move camp again to where the caribou would migrate. That was how the father would decide these things for his family. The father or eldest would be the head of the family only to his own children or siblings. Today the mayor has too many responsibilities, because he decides for the whole settlement, for all the people. It was easier then to be a manager then, because he represented only a few Inuit.

Being a manager has changed quite a lot, so it is doubtful if we will ever go back to that way of life. There are a few things that we must hold onto from our way of life. The parents have to continue being the head of their families. We did not have many things to go wrong then because there were no Qallunaat, no police or judges then.

Blohm
If someone did something wrong then, how was that taken care of?

Pirjuaq
Those things were not a part of our life then; but

if anything showed that a young person might be liable to do something that was not right, the elder or the oldest child in that family would scold that person that he was doing what was not right, that he was not to do that, whatever it might be. Even though the Inuit had no written laws, they had a way to govern their lives. They knew that if they did something that wasn't right they would be admonished either by their father or their oldest sibling.

In those times there were no RCMP or social workers, nor were there any judges, so the parents were the ones responsible for their children's behaviour and how they lived their lives. Inuit, even though they did not approve of some young person, did not say or do anything about it because he or she had his or her own parents or older sibling to correct him. That is how the Inuit lived peacefully before there were people who took care of those things as they do now. The eldest child in the family or the elder of the family looked out for the rest in their household. If it were not like that, the children would have led senseless lives.

The reason why we have to know how to make warm caribou clothing is that someone froze to death. It wouldn't have happened if he had worn caribou clothes, because he did not go far from the settlement. These are the things that both men and women should still know how to do.

Thinking about the future, there are some things wrong with the rules and laws, not big mistakes, but small ones. We have no doubt now that we will get Nunavut [the eastern half of the Northwest Territories, declared a separate region in 1999]. The ones who negotiated for the creation of Nunavut region can now be educated on how to run it. One of my concerns is about the future: parents with school-age children or grandchildren really should encourage them to continue their education. It will

be better for our way of life, because things have changed a lot already, and with the final agreement being reached for the creation of Nunavut, life will change again. Because today we use a lot of money and will use money even more in the future, it would be better for those attending schools to continue their education.

Nunavut means that this land belongs to all the Inuit. It's not just a large mass of land, it's ours, and Inuit will have to get educated for running Nunavut. It has happened in the past that they tried to employ Inuit to manage, but because of lack of education, their rightful places were taken by Qallunaat with more education in administration. There are too few Inuit who have university or college education, so that is one thing that will have to be corrected in the future. Any Inuk will have to learn about running his own land in the future. They are now in the process of negotiating the final agreement during this month of December 1991 in Ottawa.

There are no Inuit prepared to take on the responsibility of running Nunavut. If we do not learn to do things on our own, we will never change for the better. They are always asking for assistance, whereas if they had gotten their education they would have been able to take care of things on their own. There are just a handful of Inuit people who have completed their education. Inuit are behind in everything, because of their lack of education. The ITC (Inuit Tapirisat of Canada) and TFN (Tungavik Federation of Nunavut) organizations have been negotiating with the federal government for almost 15 years now, and we have been getting impatient. But now, too, we are taken by surprise that they have made a final agreement when we aren't prepared to take on the responsibilities. Now that the final agreement has been reached, we will be given the responsibilities that come with getting our

Nunavut region. I'm sure that TFN will support the Inuit when they take the responsibilities on. But we have not got the education for managing our land. You need education do those things involved in running Nunavut.

Here in our household, our meals are different from each other. My wife and I eat more caribou meat than our children, who prefer store-bought food. I feel that in future generations, when we, the elder people, have passed on, they will eat meals that are mostly store-bought, and not too much wildlife meat. And if that is the way it is then, they will use a lot more money than we do now. We already feel that we use too much money to supplement our wildlife catch of caribou and fish. So if future generations are going to eat mostly store-bought foods, then they really should finish their education. Because we already supplement store-bought foods with wildlife catch. Here in Baker Lake you used to get most things free of charge. For example, when you asked to be taken to our house from uptown by skidoo you did not worry about having to pay. Whereas in the south even if you are not going very far you have to pay to be taken there. In this area too, I feel that Inuit will soon be doing the same thing, paying for every little thing, having to pay for things we want or need even if it does not belong or seem right in our way of life. Because we need so much money now to survive, having a university or college education has become so very important, and I fully encourage it.

The final agreement for the creation of Nunavut has been reached before all our wildlife has been killed off, which I am very happy about, so that the animals can be conserved. What I do not like about this is that the Inuit who could have taken over the work in the offices do not have the education to do so. If they were to hire an Inuk to be a wildlife officer, he could approach an elder for advice on how we conserved and protected our wildlife; which I feel is good, but though some Inuit have some education they do not have the qualifications needed to work in an office, because just being able to talk in English isn't enough, you need to be able to write as well.

I myself, if someone spoke to me in English asking me to do something, I would eventually understand; but I would never understand the written stuff or be able to write in English. ITC approached us Inuit with a question: "After the creation of Nunavut region, what will Inuit become?" Then ITC answered, "We will be Canadian."

So if we are to be Canadian, the leadership of Nunavut and the government will have to co-operate and communicate with each other. The only way the Canadian government will be informed about the activities in the Nunavut region is to have material written in English. Because if we sent them a letter written only in Inuktitut they would not understand what is being said, because Inuit interpreter-translators are too few. And for this reason I fully encourage Inuit to get a higher education. We will have to keep the other Canadians informed on our activities in the areas of wildlife, finances, and mining. It could be that TFN would want to open a mine somewhere in Nunavut region to mine either nickel or gold. Here too Nunavut will need leadership to manage the situation.

Here in Baker Lake there are a number of Inuit who can speak English, but like myself cannot be employed in office work because they cannot write in English. We are behind when it comes to education, and we regret that our Inuit do not have the qualifications to assume such a responsibility.

Any Inuk can be a guide to southern tourists, but when it comes to being an office worker, we all have to have the training according to our abilities. There are quite a few Inuit who have know-how when it comes to wildlife conservation, but we cannot make written documents, so we can only pass on our knowledge by word of mouth.

I am happy about the final agreement having been reached before all our caribou have been killed off because of mining activities, and we Inuit have been given an opportunity to be involved in managing our land. But even so I think it will be hard to find someone who qualifies, and I am sure that TFN will support getting someone in to be a leader. That is one of my concerns for the future.

For the future, there are two main things that the Inuit will have to know how to do. Because our weather can be very harsh, women will still have to learn how to make caribou skin clothing and the men will have to have the knowledge to travel even in bad weather. Another thing is that the Inuit will have to have higher education.

Blohm

Are those all your hopes and concerns for the future, or do you have something to add?

Pirjuaq

Yes, I do have something to add. Inuit lives are bound by law. For instance, some parents are never informed beforehand when their own son will be taken to court. What I would like to see in the future is that the traditional way of life of the Inuit be known — how parents raised their families and managed their households. With the creation of Nunavut region, the traditional way of dealing with problems that arise should be brought back to some degree, with the help of the parents, and the young people recognizing their parents as heads. The young people need to realize that they should listen to their fathers and mothers. Those are some of the things I would like to see instilled in young people's minds.

Perhaps in this way the justice system would not be so overloaded with cases, because there would be fewer young people breaking the law, because the parents would have taken more control of how their young people live. Yesterday, today, and tomorrow again they will be holding court cases in Baker Lake. But the thing is that not even the parents know why their children are in court. For this reason the parents have to take control of their children's lives. Especially now that we have Nunavut. It is about time that we instill our values in our young people's minds, so that in the future when they themselves become parents they too will teach their children Inuit values.

That is especially important because our population has grown a lot compared to the time when we first moved to the settlement. At one time the younger generation recognized the fact that they should listen to their parents, and we, the elder Inuit whose ages range from 50 to 60 years of age, knew that we had respected and listened to our fathers and siblings. It's only recently that the younger children stopped being taught to respect and listen to their parents and older siblings. I think the reason is that they have been taught that school principals have to be shown more respect. If a student has done something that isn't right in school, he has not done something against the law; parents always knew enough to respect the law. With the creation of Nunavut region, the fact that the younger people have to recognize parents as authorities has to be included. If we could only get back the respect we used to have for our parents. That is one thing that we really have to get back in our lives. But there are some things that we do not want to go back to because they made life too difficult.

Blohm

After the Inuit were brought into the settlement of Baker Lake, were they forced to start making carvings, even though they did not really want to?

Pirjuaq

Yes. What I have heard is that the Baffin Island region people had been doing carvings for a long time, but we from the Baker Lake area were late in starting. When the Inuit started gathering in the settlement of Baker Lake, the number of people who needed social assistance grew, so people were tested to see who could do carvings, and it turned out that some people were hesitant to ask for welfare assistance because they were told that they weren't even trying to make any money, or that they didn't even try to carve.

Here in Baker we did not start making any carvings until the 1960s, after we had heard that the Baffin Inuit had been making carvings for a while to make money and that we could make good money by making carvings out of soapstone. The making of carvings is quite new to inland Inuit.

Right now we do not have a craft shop, because it wasn't making enough money, but there are people who still make carvings and make good money out of it. For example, just a few days ago I ran into Arnasugaaq, a man who likes to joke around with me. I pretended not to think too much of him, so he showed me a cheque he'd gotten for doing a carving for the co-op store. He said, "You always try to be better than I am, so as soon as I woke up this morning I started making a carving and look how much I got for it when the co-op opened." Some Inuit enjoy making carvings and you can make good money, and, like Arnasugaaq, buy skidoos and not have to depend on social assistance. But some of the elder Inuit just do not have the talent to make carvings. Arnasungaaq teased me, saying that while I, the pitiful Inuk, was still asleep he made a carving and got a $300 cheque when the co-op opened. I think that making carvings will continue to be a part of our lives.

Getting married a long time ago was different from today. That is another subject I would like to talk about. Before the Qallunaat came, Inuit parents, while the babies were still being carried in an amauti, would ask the parents of baby boys or girls if they would agree to their sons' or girls' marriage when they grew up. Like for example my wife and I were an arranged marriage. If the girls' or boys' parents did not want to agree it was up to them to refuse or say that their child was already promised to someone else. The government and even the Anglican ministers have thought that marriage arrangements were and are senseless, but that is not so! Parents conferred with each other to request a daughter-in-law or son-in-law, and when they were married, after they grew up, they knew that even if they corrected the daughter-in-law or son-in-law, it would not be taken in a bad way by the parents.

The parents also knew that their daughter or son would be comfortable with the in-laws and could talk to them about anything they wanted. Couples have ever since time began got into arguments or fights. But in those days they did not divorce each other just because of a fight. The thought never even entered their minds. They had their parents to advise them, to help settle their differences. It was only the government who thought that our way of arranging marriages for our children did not make sense, that the parents had not come to a real agreement about the marriage, because it was arranged while the child was still being carried in the amauti. It is not true to say that an agreement or understanding had not been made when they were still babies. Today it is different. Now they make an agreement through the church after they have grown up, whereas it used to be that the promised couple waited to grow up, then would be married. There are quite a number of couples here in Baker Lake whose marriages were arranged from babyhood. As the children grow older, the father left things up to the mother when it came to arranging the marriage.

The mother could say, "I want my son to get married now," or "I want my daughter to get married now." The mother was the one who arranged the marriage. In those days the Inuit way of life made sense when it came to arranging marriages. There are more divorces now than there used to be, because the parents had not arranged the marriage.

I am not saying that the marriages today are worse then they used to be, but I feel that someone should do research about why there are more divorces now. I am aware that there are more problems than there used to be. For instance drugs and alcohol are too easy to get now, and that contributes to marriage break-up. I feel that someone should try to find out why there are more marriage break-ups. Maybe it's because parents are no longer taking control of who their children marry. But in a lot of marriage break-ups alcohol is involved.

Nowadays women and men just get married, even if they do not really choose their spouse, just because they do not have a home.

My concern is that the Inuit way of life, our tradition, is not well known.

We had a good way of life, where everything was in order and managed right. I am not saying that I have never seen a couple fighting. I have seen a lot of couples fight, just like they do today. But the thing is that they did not try and divorce each other then. It was not a part of our way of life. I do not know how divorcing became part of our life. Maybe there are more things now that cause problems.

Blohm

Do you think it is because you have adopted the southern way of life?

Pirjuaq

Yes, because divorcing was not part of the Inuit way of life. The Inuit way of life does not seem to make sense to others because we do not have written laws. The Qallunaat think we are ignorant. If that were so, there are diseases such as VD that the Inuit would have gotten. Such diseases are new to the Inuit. The fact that we do not have written laws does not mean we are totally ignorant, and it should not be used as evidence that we do not know how to govern our lives.

Instead they should look at how we lived our lives peacefully before the Qallunaat came. Inuit did not contract diseases that infect them through sexual intercourse then, because they knew how to protect and manage their lives properly before the Qallunaat came. And even though they did not have written laws, they valued the health of their bodies.

The Inuit did not have a religion before the Qallunaat came into their land, so they did not have prayers that involved all Inuit. But the Indians do have their own way of praying. The Inuit forgot who created the earth, people, and animals; that is their ignorance. It is a fact that the Inuit always knew how to take care of their health and every area of their way of life. That is another of my concerns: I do not want it to be doubted that the Inuit can manage on their own. I do not want anyone to think

we will be incapable of managing Nunavut. Maybe they will feel incapable once Nunavut policy has been implemented if small changes are made to Nunavut policy. But TFN is quite capable, and they will be requesting that Nunavut region become a province. But they might be hesitant to request that each community have its own government, because they might be refused, because it might be felt that the Inuit will not be able to manage on their own. But we can say that we would be able to run Nunavut if we do become a province, because Inuit have always known how to manage their lives.

In the past, Inuit did not get married right off the bat. When the child got to be a certain age, the person who thought she would make a nice daughter-in-law would ask, and the child's parents would reply that she had already been promised to someone else, and once the boy's parents understood that, they would leave it alone.

What I find very difficult to talk about is the subject of divorce, because we Inuit did not divorce before; it is new to us. It was not until I became an elderly man that I started seeing Inuit divorcing, because it wasn't part of the Inuit way of life before. Maybe the reason for divorcing now is that they both make incomes now. I don't know, but there are so many things in our lives now that we did not have before. In those days before the Qallunaat came, the only way for my wife and I to survive was to help each other. Maybe that was the reason why we never even thought about divorcing. Today if a couple divorce, they do not feel that either of them will have trouble surviving, because they can both be employed. I really don't know what is causing so many divorces.

The Inuit always knew how to manage their lives — marriage and every area of their lives. And

because they did not write down their laws, they lived their lives according to unwritten laws they kept in their minds. They were told to always make others feel welcome, even the people who came from far away. And though those things were not written down, they were taught to the children, how they should live their lives. When Qallunaat first started to arrive, they found that Inuit are a very friendly people, so they did not fear for their lives or feel unwelcome. Inuit will always be friendly, because it is in their nature and character. The type of person you are, whether you are friendly or unfriendly, depends upon your nature, not anything else. If a person who is already unfriendly is told over and over to be friendly, she will never become friendly, because it isn't in her nature. It's like wolves: they are vicious because that is the way they are. Marriages were arranged then in a proper way, not without thought.

And if you have any further question, I think that is all I have to say. I have covered every area. The parents have to be recognized and respected by their children, because young people who, if they had lived within their mother's rules, respecting and recognizing her role in their lives, would not have needed to appear in court, now have to appear before a judge.

Harry, in check jacket, seated admist his people in a Fullerton snowhouse. The photograph is from Captain Bernier's album and was probably made by Captain Comer.

THE NATIONAL ARCHIVES OF CANADA, C1516 — J.E. BERNIER COLLECTION.

INTRODUCTION TO ZEBEDEE NUNGAK

On a bitterly cold night in January 1992, while flying to Inukjuaq, in Nunavik, on the western coast of Hudson Bay, I talked to Zebedee Nungak, Vice-President of Makivik Corporation and chair of the Inuit Justice Task Force, during a stopover in the airport at Salluit, a small settlement on Hudson Strait. My recent experience with the white Canadian justice system in Baker Lake in December 1991 and the death of Armand Tagoona were vivid in my mind.

I value Nungak's healthy disrespect for the dominant society. Never hurtful, he is certainly never afraid to speak his mind, with force and humour. He is always ready with a smile. One might say that he is the Inuit's Inuk. The autobiographical essay that follows will explain why. **HB**

LIFE AMONG THE QALLUNAAT: THREE LIFETIMES IN ONE

Zebedee Nungak

At the age of forty, I feel that I have lived three lifetimes! Each encompassed a very specific span of time, with its own characteristics and defining moments. This experience is at once dizzying, exhilarating, wrenching, stimulating, overwhelming, and, in many ways, very difficult to describe.

My people were still very nomadic and living the traditional ways when I was born at our clan camp in Saputiligait, forty miles south of Povungnituk. Until I was twelve, I grew up in an environment with a very strong Eskimo identity. I spoke only Inuktitut, as did 99.9 percent of my people. We may have been poor in material ways, but we were rich culturally. We had a strong sense of adequacy, confidence, and self-esteem, which characterized life within family and clan units.

This started to change with the coming of government to our land.

Life had not changed so radically when the only Qallunaat were those in the Hudson's Bay Company, and an occasional RCMP officer. With the establishment of schools and of a permanent government presence in our homelands, our traditional patterns of life changed forever. Those of us who were children in this period became the preoccupation of people other than our parents. These were teachers, foreigners, determined to mould us into entities entirely different from what they found us to be.

At this time Qallunaat seemed almighty in so many ways! Their technology was wondrous. They could fly airplanes and talk to each other over vast distances on radio. They lived in warm wooden houses and seemed to lack no material thing. All their women seemed to be beautiful. Their food was the envy of all during my childhood and seemed to be what the word delicious was invented for. Even their garbage was good!

My innocent ambition became to be like them. If I could not become a Qallunaat, I was determined to do the next best thing. I would learn their language and live their lifestyle. The measure of my success would be when my garbage would be as good as theirs.

I embarked on this journey at the age of twelve, and so started a second life. The federal government had a policy of sending "bright young Eskimos" to school in the south.

I had learned enough English in school to carry on a functional conversation. I was considered bright, so the government was determined to "educate" me into someone who could be useful in the modern, changing world. For the next seven years I lived as a Qallunaat, and this changed my world forever.

Living among them for so long, I learned that Qallunaat were not so almighty. Their wondrous technology could cost many lives, as well as save them. It turned out that not all lived in good houses. Many of them were poor and homeless. And hungry! Their women were not all beautiful. Their food became tiresome and not as good as our fish, seal, and caribou. Even their garbage was picked over and eaten by the unfortunate among them. My mental images of a perfect Qallunaat world were thoroughly shattered during those years. But I did learn their language. And I lived enough of their lifestyle to do me for a lifetime.

During the later part of my time among the Qallunaat, I experienced a primal hunger and an

Dan Cadzow's store with mink furs. In front, Peter Timble and Jacob Njooth. New Rampart House, Yukon Territories.

PHOTOGRAPH BY ALASKA AND CANADA COLLECTION — NATIONAL ARCHIVES OF CANADA, 653156 — ALASKA AND POLAR REGIONS DEPT. UNIVERSITY OF ALASKA FAIRBANKS.

eager thirst for my roots as an Inuk. I came to detest the deprivation of family, language, and culture that this exercise was costing me.

My brief employment with the government almost turned me into a vegetable. The facility in English that I attained during my time in the south, I realized, I could not use properly simply by acting as a servant for the government. I would use it instead serving my people, the Inuit. Thus ended my life among the Qallunaat.

I returned north to be among my people again, and I was at long last home. Profound changes had taken place during my absence. Established villages had replaced the traditional camps, and our people had congregated and become townspeople. They had gathered, most reluctantly, in order to be near their children, who had to attend school. The government now enjoyed ease of administering the Eskimos. Improvements to transportation and communications gradually evaporated the isolation that had insulated our language and culture from the march of civilization. My people had developed a political awareness that moved them to challenge many activities of different levels of government.

Many others of my contemporaries had learned the languages of the Qallunaat too. It was into this sort of ferment that I full-heartedly plunged my energies as a young adult.

I embarked on another lifetime, representing my people in the political world. My appetite for rediscovering my roots and identity as an Inuk was being satisfied at the same time as my knowledge of English was coming in handy for my people.

My knowledge of English was, of course, useless when I was on the floe edge hunting seal or participating in the butchering of a good catch of walrus. But my rediscovered skills in being an Inuk man were never useless when meeting with prime ministers and premiers for the sake of my people.

I have participated in many profoundly challenging issues, and helped lead the Inuit in dealing with them: the negotiations for the James Bay and Northern Quebec Agreement, the conferences of Aboriginal Constitutional Issues, the promotion of self-government rights for my people. In all these efforts, I have felt the spirit of our sivulliviniit, our ancestors. It remains in us to give us strength. If it were not for this, we could not face the baffling and sometimes insidious challenges we are often confronted with.

I feel myself to be the property of my people. I could not lease my experience or abilities to others, even if I were to be a poor man materially. I am an Inuk, and immensely proud to be one. My hope for the remainder of my life is that I can instill that pride in my own children. And I will trust the spirit of my ancestors to get us through whatever this life will throw at us.

SECOND INTRODUCTION TO ZEBEDEE NUNGAK

Here is Zebedee Nungak's presentation, as Chairman of the Inuit Justice Task Force, to the November 1992 National Round Table on Justice Issues for the Royal Commission on Aboriginal Peoples.

JUSTICE AMONG THE INUIT

Zebedee Nungak

The radical transformation of Inuit life in the Arctic that has transpired in the past forty years can lead the uninformed to the erroneous conclusion that Inuit did not possess a justice system before contact with European civilization. That our people led a nomadic existence in a harsh, unforgiving Arctic environment may lead Qallunaat or others to conclude that Inuit did not have a sense of order, a sense of right or wrong, or a way to deal with wrongdoers in their society.

Inuit did possess a sense of order and of right and wrong. The way it was practised and implemented may never have been compatible with European civilization's concepts of justice, but what worked for Inuit in their environment was no less designed for conditions of life in the Arctic than that of Qallunaat was for conditions of their life.

In the pre-contact period, Inuit lived in camps set up according to the seasons and the availability of life-sustaining wildlife. Their leadership was entrusted to the elders of the camp, as well as the hunters who were the best providers and who were followed for their ability to decide for the clan or group where the best areas were to spend the seasons. The overriding concern was the sustenance of the collective.

Any dispute among the people was settled by the elders or leaders, who always had the respect and high regard of the group. The decisions of these people, who were the wise and experienced of the clan, were always respected and abided by. In the rare cases where this was not the case (where an offender refused to obey the sanctions imposed by the leadership), extreme measures were taken. If the offense was serious enough to disrupt the constant struggle for life, and the person who caused that disruption made clear his refusal to obey what was imposed on him, the leadership often resolved to kill the offender. Our oral tradition is rich with stories of such episodes, where somebody was killed by sanction of the leadership.

It should be said immediately that such cases were the exception and not the rule. Then again, everything humanly possible was done to advise the culprit to mend his ways or to follow the decision of the leadership before such a radical measure was carried out.

The bulk of disputes handled by the traditional ways in the pre-contact period involved providing practical advice and persuasive exhortation for correct and proper behaviour, which were generally accepted and abided by. In more serious cases, offenders were ostracized or banished from the clan or group. In these cases, the ostracized or banished individuals were given no choice except to leave the security and company of the group that imposed this sentence. The social stigma of having such a sentence imposed was often enough to reform or alter the behaviour that was the original cause of this measure, and people who suffered this indignity once often became useful members of society, albeit with another clan in another camp.

Our oral tradition abounds with stories of such people, who went on to lead lives useful to their fellow Inuit as providers, and, in some cases, leaders of their groups or clans. It can be said that Inuit were completely self-sufficient in this aspect of their lives, as they were in every other respect prior to the arrival in their homeland of other people.

This was the practice when Inuit culture was still untouched by outside influences, when the culture and language were vigorous. Inuit possessed a very strong sense of adequacy, which was honed by the constant struggle for survival in the most unforgiving and harsh climate on earth. Survival and sustenance of the collective were the primary factors that dictated the decisions of the system of justice and dispute resolution.

There was, moreover, no question about who had the responsibility to make such decisions. The elders and the most able providers were the undisputed leaders and arbiters for resolving conflict when it arose in the traditional life of the Inuit.

DISPLACEMENT OF INUIT TRADITIONS: CONTACT WITH "CIVILIZATION"

When authorities of the government of Canada, represented by the Royal Canadian Mounted Police, became the chief arbiters of justice among the Inuit, traditional methods and customs were immediately and completely displaced by a new order. The King's or Queen's authority, represented by the police and courts, became the only system of justice. There was no place for Inuit traditions, and neither was there any regard for how things were done before. An utterly foreign system of justice was imposed upon the Inuit, and the role of the elders and leaders was rendered useless.

The new representatives of British justice totally ignored the values, traditions, and customs of the Inuit in their determination to have their laws obeyed.

Crown law (the Wishes of the Great White Monarch for His Subjects), only vaguely or not at all understood by Inuit, became supreme. The case of Sinnisiak and Uluksak, chronicled in the book *British Law and Arctic Man*, is a case in point.

The formality and circumstance surrounding the administration of British justice in the Arctic clashed violently with the traditional Inuit notion of justice.

Whereas dispute resolution had been based on the well-being of the collective, and was dispensed by those who were morally, if not legally, well regarded by their society, it was now handled by foreigners, strangers who spoke a strange language. The roles of the judge, jury, prosecutor, and defence were for a long time beyond the comprehension of subjects who lived in the Arctic.

The Inuit and their interpreters, even if they were competent, struggled mightily with concepts such as due process, individual rights, juries, appeals, and such untranslatables as "guilty" and "not guilty."

Moreover, the Inuit as a nation, or a distinct collective of people, had absolutely no role in the formulation of the laws they were expected to live under as Canadian citizens. These laws were made by people sitting in a faraway legislature who were just as ignorant of Inuit society as we were of Qallunaat society. The loss of enablement and the sense of inadequacy were made more complete by the fact that justice was now dispensed by people who showed up so infrequently that it was difficult to maintain a sense of who these remote authorities really were.

PARTICIPATION ON THE FRINGES: INUIT IN THE JUSTICE SYSTEM

With the passage of time and the advent of education among our people, Inuit eventually became involved in the outer periphery of the legal system, other than being the accused. Many became policemen, interpreters, and, in later years, court workers and cor-

rectional officers. This has taken place without the legal system's being "aboriginalized," that is, without all levels of the system, foreign as it is to Inuit, being deliberately programmed to be manned by Inuit. It is still essentially a system completely foreign to Inuit values.

But even with its inherent inadequacies, Inuit have made small inroads as participants on the fringes of the justice system. In the fields where they work at present, Inuit personnel have proven themselves competent, and in many cases indispensable to the justice system. Their facility in the language and knowledge of the culture of their people have made them vitally necessary to the function and integrity of the legal system. As policemen, they are preferred by far over non-Inuit, as they are as interpreters and court workers.

LACK OF INUIT CONTROL: A FUNDAMENTAL FLAW

It hardly needs to be restated that pre-contact self-sufficiency was ripped out and replaced with a system that neither integrated nor took into consideration the pre-existing values, norms, and concepts of justice of the Inuit. Before any serious attempt is made to examine what those norms and concepts were, the question of lack of control by Inuit of the justice system has to be first addressed. What is the use of studying values that were discarded, ignored as irrelevant, or otherwise swamped by the imposition of a totally foreign justice system if that system will continue to operate and exist under complete and total control of the dominant society? Why go through the agony of enumerating these values if the dominant authorities will be the only ones picking and choosing which ones are compatible and which ones are not? To spare us the futility of such an exercise, we first have to be provided with an answer to these fundamental questions: To what degree will Inuit have control over the justice system in their ancestral homeland? How much self-government will be accorded to facilitate this dream?

Once these questions are adequately answered, it would take a series of in-depth ethnological and anthropological studies to do justice to the fundamental values, norms, and concepts that the present system presumes to want to know about. But until then, we have to be wary and genuinely sceptical about getting drawn into an exercise that will come to naught if the administration and implementation of the system remains firmly in the hands of foreigners who will never have an adequate appreciation and respect for Inuit values.

FUNDAMENTAL REFORM VERSUS TINKERING

Upon closer examination of this issue, it will certainly be found that many cultural differences exist between Inuit and western society. Because some differences will appear to be irreconcilable, a question will rise about whether Inuit traditional law can or should be applied in the contemporary world. There will be a question as to whether, on the one hand, Inuit should have a completely separate justice system, or, on the other, our values can be integrated and adapted as amendments to the existing system of laws.

Is the present system flexible enough to allow the accommodation of what appear to be cultural incompatibilities? Will the system endure encroachment upon its well-established traditions to

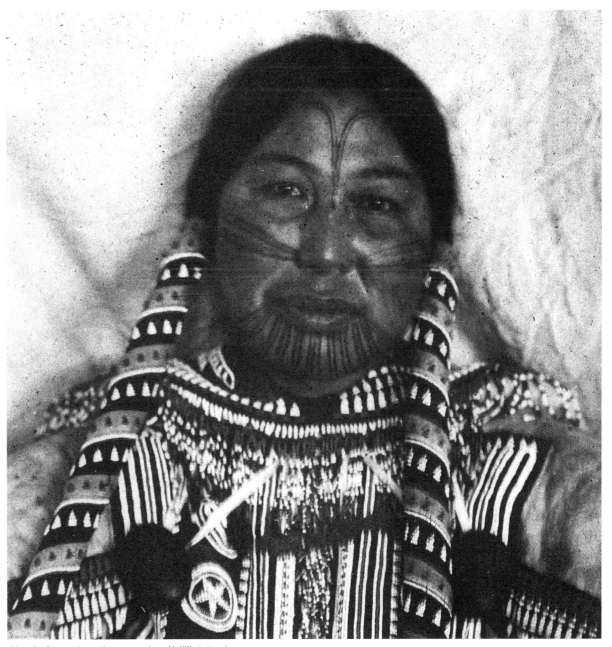

Shoofly Comer in native war paint. Aivillik tattooing.

PHOTOGRAPH ATTRIBUTED TO A.P. LOW — COURTESY OF NATIONAL ARCHIVES, C86032 — UNIVERSITY OF OTTAWA CENTRAL LIBRARY COLLECTION.

A dignified portrait of "She-nuck-shoo, Chief of the Ivalik." He was also known, aboard the whaler *Era*, as Harry (native name "Tsenueke" in Captain Comer's diary.)

PHOTOGRAPH BY GERALDINE MOODIE — PHOTO CREDIT TO THE R.C.M.P. MUSEUM — REGINA, SASK.

integrate aspects of a culture, language, and lifestyle foreign to itself?

At what point would acceptable tinkering be regarded as unacceptable radical surgery? These are questions for which there will have to be answers. Whatever changes may be required to achieve acceptable co-existence, it is certain that a fundamental reform is necessary in the relationship between Inuit and non-Inuit society. If tinkering with the existing system cannot satisfy identified needs, then a thorough, fundamental reform has to be contemplated. For this, a bold will and willingness will have to be mustered by the powers of the dominant society, qualities that it has yet to demonstrate toward aboriginal people. The aboriginal Constitutional Conferences of the 1980s, the debacle of the Meech Lake Accord, and the failure of the Charlottetown Agreement all attest to this.

Fundamental values, norms, and concepts of justice of the Inuit? Let us be shown by what means we would be empowered to put them into practice before we volunteer these to you. We may be a square peg unable to fit into your round hole!

SECOND INTRODUCTION TO ALOOTOK IPELLIE

Like the other writers in this book, Alootook Ipellie speaks as a witness to a human tragedy, yet the proud people he speaks for have roots strong enough to withstand the withering effects of colonialism. Their hope for the future is expressed in this poem. **HB**

JOURNEY TOWARD POSSIBILITIES

Alootook Ipellie

Nothing should be left to an invaded people except their eyes for weeping.
— *Otto von Bismarck*

Like Mary
My mother and father created
An immaculate conception.
Well, almost.
Who in his right mind would think
He was immaculate?
There are plenty of souls out there
Who will make such a confession.
Woebegone to this vulnerable world.
Nothing immaculate in what I
See, hear, feel, taste or smell.
But I have always expected immaculateness
Ever since being able to comprehend
My fellow man's outpourings.
But as these years pass by
My great disappointment is still endless.
Man's penchant for immaculate discovery
In human beings will always fail miserably
Simply because he is doomed to a
Finite failure.
Civilization in its very nature is violent
And we are but a small portion
Of its victims.
Also it can be said that
Because of man's violent nature
We, as a distinct entity
Have survived obliteration
For now.
Manipulation has played a central role

Within our side of the world
The circumpolar world.

But to manipulate men,
to propel them toward goals
which you — the social reformers —
see, but they may not, is to
deny their human essence,
to treat them as objects without
will of their own, and therefore
to degrade them.*

Our homelands have been stamped
With these very words
For as long as dominators
Of dominant societies
Have dominated us.
Unfortunately for the foreseeable future
These very words will remain
Comfortably cemented.
Unless a new era dawns
In our circumpolar world
A yearning not quite like any
Other hunger is growing
Along with a desire
To break away from the grasp
Of colonialism.
So we may once again squire dignity
Within our hearts and minds
And replenish our souls with pride.
Until we are given back our
Lost pride and dignity
We shall drape indignation
On all those who
Enjoy our friendliness
And the splendour of our homelands
Until these chains tied

* Sir Isaiah Berlin, Fellow of All Souls, Oxford University.

Around our will are removed forever.
We as a collective
Will continue to be denied
Our freedom.
Allow us to imagine that
Wonderful state of mind
When ecstasy runneth over
Our goose pimples
In the final realization
Of our greatest desire
To be freed from
Our dominators' cage.
The hand that may well
Secure our freedom
Is contained in the
Embodiment of a new
Arctic Policy
For our circumpolar world.
Our greatest hopes
Have found a perfect
Gilded foundation
On which to build a protective structure
For our people's continued existence
As a distinct entity
In this global cultural mosaic.
Since many of our cherished dreams
Still fade unfulfilled
We are determined as ever
To embark on a journey
Toward possibilities
For our people
And our homelands.

Godspeed.

Geraldine Moodie's favourite model, the deaf and dumb woman
"Koo-tuck-tuck" gazes out shyly at the camera.

PHOTOGRAPH BY GERALDINE MOODIE. —
PHOTO CREDIT TO THE R.C.M.P. MUSEUM — REGINA, SASK.

FIRST INTERLUDE

Hans-Ludwig Blohm

The signing of the Gwich'in Indian Land Claim Settlement on 22 April 1992 in Fort McPherson, Northwest Territories was to take place during three days of feasting and festivities. I planned to attend, driving from Ottawa to Fort McPherson, and from there to Tuktoyaktuk, and later into Alaska. It would be my twelfth overland trip to the Yukon and Alaska in the years between 1976 and 1992. I drove some 22,037 kilometres — and travelled many by air — between 5 April and 2 June 1992.

* * *

Over the years I have driven several different cars. Only the Volvo 245 proved solid enough to withstand four trips. The crowning touch for this trip, my longest, was a Mazda MPV 4/4. I missed the comfort of my Volvos. For a long journey over rough roads, you need good seating if your back is to survive, and mine has!

On Sunday, 5 April 1992 I departed, alone, though on many previous trips I had had company. Usually my wife Ingeborg joined me for part of a trip. For the last big adventure we met in Vancouver to drive into the spring, back to our home in Nepean, outside Ottawa.

The route around the Great Lakes is always fascinating: the weather changes, the light changes, the seasons change. The first really memorable event of this trip happened near Lanigan, Sakatchewan. There I saw geese by the hundred of thousands. It was springtime in the prairies, and they were migrating north, just like me. Huge flocks wove back and forth through the evening sky in what

seemed like disorder, but soon they assumed formations, which rose higher and higher, then they dropped down to the fields to feed on the remains of last year's harvest. Most of the snow had melted and some sloughs were free of ice. It was a sight to behold. My Leica cameras saw a lot of action.

After Edmonton and Dawson Creek it was on to the Alaska Highway, which I had travelled many times, even before the Second World War military road was upgraded. As usual, I stopped at the Liard River Hot Springs to soak myself. Later, in Whitehorse, I looked into the Archives for historical photographs. A day of rest at the home of my good friend Dr. Helmut Schoener in Dawson City was in order. He is the area's flying dentist, and sure enough we winged our way across the mighty, mostly frozen Yukon River toward Eagle, Alaska for coffee with some friends.

On April 15, ten days out of Ottawa, I headed for the Dempster Highway. This, the most northerly all-weather road on the continent, is more alluring for me than the Alaska Highway. I borrowed an extra gas tank from the McGillivrys, proprietors of the large Esso station at the beginning of the Dempster, with whom I had come to feel at home. The weather was great — blue sky, sunshine, a little wind, and moderate temperatures.

I planned to head straight to Inuvik in the Northwest Territories, and, weather permitting, carry on over the Mackenzie River ice road to Tuktoyaktuk. The unpredictability of the weather is the great unknown. I knew from experience that the weather in the Dempster region changes rapidly.

It was great crossing the continental divide at North Fork Pass, and then climbing into the Ogilvie Mountains. The views into the Tombstone Valley and the Blackstone River under blue skies were a photographer's delight. A big moose crossed the

road in the distance. I could only get a shot of the fresh tracks. Much later, on the Eagle Plains, I spotted a grizzly trying to get into another animal's hole. It got wind of me faster than I could grab the Leica. Off it took, without a second glance.

In late afternoon, about 50 kilometres south of the Arctic Circle, the weather changed: windclouds in the far distance, drifting snow. I was not surprised to find the big red lights blinking at the Eagle Plains Hotel to signal that the road was closed

It was coffee time. The talk was all about the road ahead. Would the bulldozers be able to clear the road through the Richardson Mountains? Time was money for the big rigs. I had not encountered any vehicles on the 350 kilometres from the cut-off at the Klondike Highway. Here was the explanation.

At that latitude in the middle of April, daylight hours are already getting longer. Everybody was keen to move, to reach Inuvik for the night. After several hours the all clear was given. The big rigs roared to life, stirring up huge clouds of light snow. I did not want to be caught between these giants, convoy fashion, so I let them move out, one after another. I had filled my gas tank to the brim and was ready to go when the last big guy was at a respectable distance. I did not want to be hampered by smaller cars and pick-ups, so I waited, ready for my time to move out.

And move I did, feeling jubilant. The open metal grid decking of the famous bridge at Eagle River rang with its distinctive sound. A new solid structure marked the Arctic Circle where a big truck tire used to hang on a makeshift wooden tripod. I remembered that in the summer of 1979 I had taken a photograph of my travelling companion, former German Ambassador to Canada Rupprecht von Keller, poking his grinning face through the tire.

The McPherson R.C.M.P. Patrol that travelled Dawson to McPherson and back again. Left to right: Indian Peter, Constable Pasley, Staff Sergeant Dempster, Indian Jimmy, and Constable Tyack.

PHOTOGRAPH BY C. TIDD. TAKEN MARCH 19, 1920 — YUKON ARCHIVES, WHITEHORSE, 7291 — C. TIDD COLLECTION.

hundred pies for the festivities. I tried some later. Absolutely delicious!

Once the green light appeared on the big sign beside the road, all the trucks and cars roared to life with a cacophony of sound. Diesel engines with turbo chargers belched huge clouds of black smoke. Smaller cars had to be cleared of ice and snow. I had kept my Mazda van in readiness, so I was on the road again in no time. I let the big rigs move out first to flatten out the new snowdrifts. During some of my photo stops other cars pulled ahead of me, but after I crossed into the Northwest Territories I met them all again, lined up on a long straight stretch of road. One could just make out some mountains in the far distance, beyond the next valley. At the bottom of the valley we could see what the trouble was: a big rig and a maintenance snowblower straddled the snow-packed road.

We had to wait hours before a big Cat arrived to rescue us. It went up and down the incline a couple of times to break the hard-packed snow and ice with its big cleats. Very slowly the tractor-trailer was freed and pulled up the hill. Meanwhile, some of the more impatient southbound vehicles tried to pass the Cat with the rig in tow. Despite snow-chains, none made it up the hill. It was a nightmare, a direct result of stupidity. The Cat had to pull all of them out of the way before returning to the task of getting the Big One up the hill. Some fun!

Our long convoy of trucks, pickups, vans, and cars dispersed after the road was clear. Crossing the

As I moved into the Richardson Mountains, the wind was blowing snow onto the highway. I encountered a drift that pushed me helplessly off the road onto the earthen berm. The snow was so deep I couldn't open my door until a passing driver got me out. It took a snow removal Cat to wrestle the car back on the road. A swig of coffee from my big thermos set me up to continue north. But the road ahead was declared closed again. The order came via radio phone to return, convoy fashion, to the Eagle Plains Hotel.

Meanwhile, the sun had hit the horizon and the wind had started to blow with great fury. We spent two and a half days at the hotel. All traffic that had already passed the Dempster cut-off at the Klondike

Highway ended up there, the only shelter along the entire 750 kilometres between the Klondike Highway and Inuvik in the north.

My short photographic stop at the Arctic Circle cost me a forced rest I could ill afford, both in time and money. But such is life in the unpredictable north. The time passed with good long sleeps, eating, writing, laundry, and photographing other stranded hotel guests.

One of the guests, a Gwich'in Indian elder woman, was also travelling to the big signing ceremony. She worked at the Tourist Centre in Carcross in the Yukon. They expected that hundreds of Gwich'in would appear at Fort McPherson for the big event. She was going to bake more than two

A view of men dressed up for a Potlatch at Alaska.

Front kneeling: Edward Wood
Front row from l to r: Paul Chancy, Pat Henry (Hayes), Charlie Steve, Billy Silas, Harpe, David Taylor, David Roberts, Peter son (Chief Jousse's brother)
Back row from l to r: Kenith, Chief Alex, Johnathan Johnson, Canadian Joe, Esaw Harpe, Drew Silas, Chief Isaac, and Gone Hawk is flags dancing.

PHOTOGRAPH NO. 5781 – YUKON ARCHIVES, WHITEHORSE, 5781 – KATES COLLECTION.

Peel and Mackenzie River ice bridges was easy. I arrived at the hotel in Inuvik shortly before midnight, in pitch darkness. A light snow was falling again. It felt bloody good to get out of my van.

Walter Wilkomm, my host, was waiting. I had never met him or his charming wife Hildegard. She brewed some real Bremer Kaffee — named after Bremen, Walter's hometown in Germany — for me before she retired. Walter and I sat in the deserted bar till the wee hours of the morning, discussing, philosophizing. It was an absolute delight.

After sleeping in and eating a good solid breakfast, I departed for Aklavik, a settlement of equal numbers of Gwich'in Indians and Inuvialuit, as the Eskimos call themselves in the western Arctic. This 50-50 mix, with a sprinkling of whites, appears to be functioning reasonably well. However, Aklavik had not been on my agenda. I had not known that it was connected via ice road to Inuvik, as is Tuktoyaktuk. Walter recommended a visit, since the natives there were holding their annual spring festival. It was an overcast day for my first drive on the solid, but by no means smooth, Mackenzie River ice road.

It was a unique experience. Some stretches of the metre-thick ice were snow-covered, others smooth and slick, and its hues were varied — blue, green, and milky. I stopped often to take photographs.

Some stops, though, were simply the result of long slitherings.

Traffic was almost non-existent. I had covered the 125 kilometres in reasonable time when I drove up a ramp from the riverbed to the town site. There was lots of activity on the ice below the bank, with scores of cars, tents, and people.

I had to find a place to park and get an overview of the situation. I found a spot for the car, which promptly sank into the ditch. A husky fellow came over, and after sharing a good laugh, we chatted about the North, and Aklavik in particular, and extricated the car. He turned out to be of Danish-Inuit mixed blood, Knut Hansen, whose name Walter Wilkomm had given me. Furthermore, he had

been to my home town, Rendsburg, which is just south of the Danish border.

Eventually I got onto the ice to mingle with the happy crowd. It was cold, though the sun was still up. The northern twilight hours lingered on and on. Aklavik is the only hamlet with such a mix of the two culturally distinct people. I had a hard time knowing who was Gwich'in and who was Inuvialuit.

I had some good "country food" from the various tents, as well as western fare. There were races, and tea-boiling and other contests. Threading a thin line through the eye of a needle with icy fingers seemed to be a favourite among the young boys and girls.

Potlach Dancers, SITKA, Alaska.

PHOTOGRAPH BY CASE AND DRAPER. TAKEN 1904 — COURTESY OF THE NATIONAL ARCHIVES, ALASKA AND POLAR REGIONS DEPT. UNIVERSITY OF ALASKA FAIRBANKS. — HISTORICAL PHOTOGRAPH COLLECTION.

83-204-199

Knut had invited me to share a big meal with him and his family, but unfortunately I had to be back in Inuvik to start out for Tuk. I planned to turn south from there on April 21, two days later, to attend the big signing ceremony. Only with good luck and good weather did I have a chance to make it.

It was smooth sailing all the way back to Inuvik. My experience and confidence on the ice grew with every kilometre. I was weary but very happy when I fell asleep that night in the Mackenzie Experience Hotel.

The next morning the sky was a brilliant blue, but it was a cold cold Easter!

Tuktoyaktuk lay about 200 kilometres ahead on the ice road. I had clear sailing on the river. The first stretch of the road I had traversed the previous day, but now I had brilliant sunshine. The ice glistened and the colour changed with the blue overhead. At first the road was lined by black spruce forest on either side. But soon the trees got smaller and eventually disappeared. I was above the tree line. The ice road followed all the meanders of the river channel on the east side of the mighty Mackenzie River delta. I had flown over it years earlier in the summertime and knew how immense it was. Now I was experiencing it in the grip of winter, though the snow had begun to melt in the south, and the river was flowing swiftly under the ice. The volume of this water could increase, and its pressure could build till the ice burst. Low sections of the road

Chief Goodlata-Tarral Siwash, Copper River Alaska.

PHOTOGRAPH BY CHARLES BUNNEL. TAKEN 1908 — COURTESY OF THE NATIONAL ARCHIVES, ALASKA AND POLAR REGIONS DEPT. UNIVERSITY OF ALASKA FAIRBANKS — CHARLES BUNNELL COLLECTION.

could be submerged under several feet of water. As I drove I heard ominous cracking sounds, and some stretches of the ice road had become slick and slippery. At one point I was almost out of control, and ended up sitting beside the road in deep snow. By the time a big supply truck heading for Tuk stopped to offer help I had managed to get myself out.

Further down the road I stopped many times. The land was flat as a pancake and covered with gleaming white snow under the immense blue northern sky. It was filled to the horizon with floating ice crystals. It was another one of the great moments of my life. It brought me down to scale. In the festive silence an indescribable feeling of awe and joy ran through me. It was a moment to share with people close to you. I felt like singing.

Opingalik, a Netsilik Eskimo, once said, "Songs are thoughts, brought forward with life's breath, when humans feel a great surge of energy flowing in them, and words will not suffice any more to express their feelings."

I also felt the truth of John Amagoalik's words about the land, and Alootook Ipellie's poems, and the thoughts and feelings expressed in Zebedee Nungak's essay. It is their land, the Arctic, and it is the land that gives life to all plant, animal, and human forms.

It is a land for all of us, and it wants to be treated with respect and dignity.

It was a powerful moment.

But I had to carry on, so I listened to some tapes my wife gave me for this trip, Beethoven, Mozart — strength and joy! — and spring coming!

Many more stops along the way gave me more chances to see, feel, and even smell the land. The shapes of the snowdrifts and the glistening snowcrystals were always changing. The angle of the light and my views of the drifts were always new and exciting. Many more photographs were taken.

At last the Tuk skyline appeared on the horizon, dominated by the old DEW line radar station towers.

I had the name and address of the mayor, Eddie Dillon, given to me in Ottawa by Rosemary Kuptana, president of the Inuit Taparisat of Canada. Through him I hoped to meet certain people and take some photographs for the *Inuktitut* magazine. I was picked up by a teenager with a snowmobile, who gave me a guided tour. I saw the many buildings, rigs, and workshops that had been abandoned by the oil exploration companies that once made this place bustle with activity. Some sad-looking ships were frozen in the harbour.

Mayor Eddie Dillon invited us — my young "guide" too — to join his family for their Easter feast. It was wonderfully easy-going and uncomplicated. The large family did not have enough room around their small kitchen table, so they simply hunkered down on the floor to enjoy the food, "country style" as well as western. A big TV was blaring all the time, along with a tape deck. Here too, as everywhere in the north, were a people in transition, friendly and open people with ready smiles. But here, too, my time was limited. I had to be back in Inuvik within 24 hours. It was crazy. But the time I had lost at the Eagle Plains Hotel and the fixed dates in Fort McPherson gave me no choice.

I also wanted to visit Emma and Fritz Feichtinger,

who were on my list of contacts. It turned out that Walter Wilkomm and Fritz Feichtinger were good friends. I explored Tuktoyaktuk on my own. It was late when I knocked at Emma and Fritz's door.

Emma is a hamlet elder with an Inuvialuit mother and a Swiss father. Fritz Feichtinger came north as to work on the DEW line. I was happy to be their guest for the night. We talked about their children and grandchildren, and out came the photo albums. There were photographs of Emma's childhood days and her family, and also a photograph of Fritz in his German paratrooper uniform from the Second World War. I was stunned to see a young guy in the familiar uniform. I had worn the German Navy uniform at about the same age. Fritz was some years my senior, so he saw far more of the war than I did. It became a very emotional evening for us.

Emma left us alone. But not before she showed me the wonderful fur parka her mother had crafted many decades ago. She let me take some photographs of her. We went outside into the late warm sunshine. It was a delight to see their faces glow with warmth and compassion for each other as they sat on their frozen drinking-water supply sled, which held crystal-clear ice from a lake some 25 kilometres away.

Fritz and I did not get much sleep that night. There were many memories to share, often speaking in our native German. We also shared our feelings for the people of the north and for this great country. We shared too our great concern about the bad influence of the white man's mercantile thinking, the legacy of the oil exploration boom, and the ensuing alcohol and drug problems, with their accompanying violence and crimes against property.

It was a somewhat sad parting from Fritz. I hope to see him and Emma again.

Now it was down to Inuvik and then to Fort

McPherson the next day. I had not known before arriving in Fort McPherson that Charlie Snowshoe was its mayor. I had encountered him in Ottawa in November 1991. A Gwich'in Indian elder, he was a member of a delegation from the Northwest Territories and the Yukon, invited to address the Standing Committee on Aboriginal Affairs concerning the large Porcupine caribou herd. This herd, named after the Porcupine River, which traversed its migration route, was of vital interest to all the natives of the region. Since time immemorial the north slope of the British Mountains in the Yukon, Alaska's Brooks Range, and especially Alaska's Arctic National Wildlife Refuge had been its calving grounds.

Now the U.S. Government, with the connivance of the current Alaska State Legislature, wanted to open up this sensitive area for oil exploration. The massive opposition to the bill from Canadian as well as U.S. environmentalists and native groups brought this controversial bill down to defeat in the U.S. Congress. Even U.S. President Bush's intervention on behalf of the oil industry was not enough to carry the day.

INTRODUCTION TO CHARLIE SNOWSHOE

The defeat of that bill happened on the very day the Canadian Aboriginal Affairs Committee listened to presentations from our native groups directly affected by the possibility of a disruption in the life cycle of the Porcupine caribou herd. All but one of these presentations were written submissions from lawyers and the like. The only oral presentation — simple, to the point, and effective — was by Charlie Snowshoe of Fort McPherson. **HB**

Alaska Native Indian working on Birchbark Canoe.

PHOTOGRAPH BY EVA ALVEY RICHARDS. NO DATE GIVEN — COURTESY OF THE NATIONAL ARCHIVES, ALASKA AND POLAR REGIONS DEPT. UNIVERSITY OF ALASKA FAIRBANKS — EVA ALVEY RICHARDS COLLECTION.

AN ORAL PRESENTATION TO THE STANDING COMMITTEE ON ABORIGINAL AFFAIRS

Charlie Snowshoe

Thank you, Mr. Chairman. I came on short notice, and I am not like these young people, who have a presentation written up. I am an old-timer and I am glad that I'm here with them.

I've been involved with these caribou management negotiations, and I have a concern like everybody else up north about the Porcupine caribou. You all heard the President [George Bush] talk the other day on the radio saying that he supports development up there.

He said development is not going to bother the Porcupine caribou.

The pipeline is set up there, and TV showed only one caribou going toward that pipeline, but making out that a whole bunch of caribou go in that area.

Last summer I made a trip up to Fairbanks, Alaska, to make a little show of the Northwest Territories being involved with the Porcupine caribou, and we were going to set up a tent on the land that we were concerned about, and put a Canadian flag up there saying we were representing Canadians to protect the Porcupine caribou. It didn't happen because of the weather. Nature was against us, but we met some people. We went to Kaktovik and met some people there, and we've heard different stories of what was happening in Point Barrow, Alaska.

I thought I would bring what I heard to your attention. It's hearsay, but if we had the money to travel around like everybody else we could go and visit these people, who are just like us, to find out more about it. We are concerned about the Porcupine caribou. We came down here to ask you for support to help us protect our caribou. I would like to say that money is a big thing for everybody. You have to make money to eat. You have to make money to live, and you have to have money in the bank for when you retire. But we still rely on nature. We still rely on the land, and we still rely on the wildlife.

The fur was taken away from us, and you yourself know how much damage has been done to my people. If the caribou is taken away from us, there is going to be more harm to my people. This is what I don't want to see happen.

I would like to say to you that we rely on the caribou, which is just like a bank to us. We have our meat. We have to go for it. We get it, and we have meat for a year. It's going to cost you more money if the damage is done to the caribou. I'll be coming to you for a welfare cheque, and we don't want to see this happen.

I am not much of a spokesperson, but I would like to bring to your attention that we need your help. I would like to say to you that when the wind damages the house of the President of the United States, out in the bush someplace, he's there to fix it. If damage is done in the area we are concerned about, the caribou can't go over there and fix it. That's the thing I thought I would bring to your attention. He can fix his house, but the caribou can't fix the land that's been damaged.

I don't like to come down here just for the ride. I'm very happy to be here with the boys. They're doing a good job. Some time this month I'll be coming back again to present to Cabinet more of the work we have done involving Porcupine caribou. Thank you very much.

SECOND INTERLUDE

Hans-Ludwig Blohm

After crossing the Peel and Mackenzie River ice bridges, where horizontally blowing snow made visibility poor, I arrived at McPherson and checked into the only available hotel, a co-op and dormitory.

I walked through the village with my cameras at the ready. Welcoming signs were attached to hydro wires across the main street. The air of expectation was quite palpable. I had a good time chatting with some kids. Eventually I ended up at the big school, which was bustling with preparations. The festivities were scheduled to start that evening with the first of three grand feasts.

The Gwich'in settlements of Aklavik, Inuvik, Arctic Red River, and Fort McPherson, the four main native centres, all contributed to the feasts. Huge quantities of food had started to arrive. Large tables in the centre of the auditorium were overflowing, and the floor around them could only be navigated with great care. Hundreds of people, young and old, filled the very big auditorium to capacity. A huge map of their Territory was stapled to the back wall of the stage. Big loudspeakers were foretelling the entertainment to come. It was to be a dry event; no alcohol whatsoever. Large kettles of hot soup appeared and the contents were distributed to everybody on the floor or chairs around the hall. There appeared to be much rejoicing. Relatives and friends met again. The elders, for whom there is tremendous respect, had special places in comfortable chairs.

Speeches were made. Fiddles were played, a legacy of early French Canadian voyageurs, picked up by the natives and transformed in their own style. Merriment was everywhere.

But I was dog-tired and could not last till the end. Mother nature nudged me to bed. After all, the next day promised the biggest events, the arrival of the minister of Indian Affairs, Tom Siddon, his dog-sled ride into town, and the signing of documents. I had to be wide awake and ready.

Tom Siddon's arrival at the outlying airport was eagerly awaited by reporters and local dignitaries. Light snow was falling under a grey sky. A team of dogs and a big sled waited at a distance. As the bright yellow Learjet came in for a landing, the dogs got excited and the musher had to rein them in firmly.

The transfer of the minister and his wife from the modern jet to the old-fashioned dog-sled went without a hitch. It seemed almost symbolic: the meeting of nature and high technology, of yesterday and tomorrow. The signing of the Land Claim Agreement would be a visible testimony to great change. With good will on all sides, it should succeed and so reconfirm the natives' inherent rights. It should restore their dignity and give them the strength to break free from the stupefying dependence on the white man's handouts.

Lots of people milled about the dignitaries as they proceeded into the Hamlet Council's spanking new building to greet the assembled elders, several of whom had been brought in from the hospital in Inuvik. Others came from their respective settlements. Two elder women proudly wore their Order of Canada. Handshakes and platitudes gave way to genuine human warmth.

In a room away from the public glare the first signing of documents took place, as well as the handing over of an initial cheque.

The ceremonial signing took place in the evening, in the festively adorned school auditorium, where an overflow audience of natives of all ages eagerly waited for the speeches to end and the big feast to begin. The formal signing at a table draped with a Gwich'in flag, with a Mountie in scarlet standing on either side, took quite some time. I found it delightful and meaningful that a number of youngsters set their hands to the documents. However, I thought the Mounties were an utterly superfluous remnant of colonialism.

The Canadian Gwich'in had invited some of their Alaskan relatives, who gave some sound advice from their perspective on the other side of the border. The border, drawn by the white conquerors, was meaningless to the natives, whose family and clan ties had been severed by artificial lines on the map. These Alaskan Gwich'in certainly felt unrestricted in their remarks, and even mocked the "Crown." The Mountie in charge frowned. Too bad my lens was not long enough to catch his expression. It told stories!

And then the feast, with dancing afterwards. Fiddles and drums, with the drums far more powerful, to the extent that they produced trance, or ecstasy. A large circle of people formed for a rhythmic dance, a mix of old and young, female and male. A second circle formed and a third. I was sitting in the middle of this swirling and stomping. The pace got faster and faster, the drumbeat louder and louder, almost to the point of frenzy. The whole building was shaking. I looked at the ceiling, at the huge wooden beams carrying the roof. I could see the balloons attached to the ceiling swaying in unison with the entranced dancers. It was a sight, sound, and feeling that will linger in my mind. Very powerful medicine indeed! As the intensity eased I mingled with the people, taking roll after roll of film with my Leicas. The faces! The faces!

The next morning I went out to some trapping cabins at the invitation of Wally and James Firth, travelling by snowmobile with a CBC video crew, crossing frozen lakes deep in snow. For the uninitiated it was rough, hanging on to a camera bag and a snowmachine while the young drivers had a field day trying to outrace each other.

It was all in fun and good spirits. The reward was hot tea in the cabin, where we saw furs of fox, lynx, and beaver. Some of the old traditions are still alive. Both James and Wally had full-time jobs in Inuvik as telephone technician and radio announcer respectively. Like them, their sons carried on the hunting and trapping.

I still wanted to visit the village of Arctic Red River, at the confluence of the Red River and the mighty Mackenzie. In winter the only road connection is across the ice; in summer it's by ferry. I had seen the red-roofed church steeple many times. I was particularly interested, having heard about the incredible alcohol problem in that 100-person settlement.

Two Christian churches, side by side, split the tiny community. I spoke first to a young couple, volunteers from Switzerland who were putting up an alcohol treatment centre. It was almost finished and already had some occupants. These cheerful and energetic young people were members of a religious group, I found out later, spreading their gospel!

I took a photograph of a derelict-looking post office, with its front door broken at the bottom and electrical wires cut above the roof, surrounded by piles of firewood and abandoned cars under the snow. I presumed it was vacant, abandoned, but an elderly native came out with mail in his hand, and another man came with mail to deliver.

I talked to the two. The elder, Hyacinthe Andre, Chief of the settlement for several decades, was retired. He considered himself just about the only healthy person in Arctic Red. He never touched alcohol. The younger man, the village teacher, offered to take me to the only store in the settlement, to get a cup of coffee. All the windows were shuttered and the door was closed tight. However, he knew how to get in. He knocked hard till the friendly face of the white storekeeper appeared. Queried as to why his small store was shuttered and locked, he had a one-word answer: Vandalism. In a village of 100 souls!

However, there were some positive signs: some new buildings and a health care facility. There was a small hotel, closed, but looking in good shape, and a big new arena, though with no sign of life. On the promontory high above the rivers' confluence stood the red-roofed church, like a beacon. For what, I wondered.

I returned to Inuvik to photograph an Inuvialuit artist and another elder, and some private houses under construction, where an all-white crew from the Yukon was working. I wondered why a local contractor was not doing the job, and why not a single native person was employed. Competition, was their answer. They certainly were operating swiftly, and knew what they were doing. Construction requirements are demanding in the Arctic, particularly with respect to insulation and, more significantly, the foundation. All wooden pilings are set into the permafrost. Holes are drilled into the ice-laden soil, and posts are set and slurried in with hot watered sand. Instant and permanent freezing is the result. Once founded deep enough, the well-conserved wood pilings should last indefinitely.

Recently a Russian crew had visited the site, flown in directly from Siberia to study the so-called "Utilydoors," the above-ground network of insulated service pipes for central heating and electricity and water. The north sets its own standards for almost all aspects of life.

My way back over the Dempster to Dawson City the next day was smooth and uneventful under mild and sunny conditions. Smooth, except that I blew a tire, ripped it to bits and pieces. I could not complain. It was the first flat in 53,000 kilometres, and the Dempster is known as a tire-eater.

Following a night in Dawson City I had hoped to cross the Yukon River ice bridge and go into Alaska via the "Top of the World Road," a spectacular drive that I have enjoyed often and at various times of the year. But it was still closed for the winter. So I made my way south to Whitehorse to pick up some processed colour film that I had left on my way north. The many bumps had shaken the car badly, so I got a new set of tires and some needed servicing for my Mazda MPV. I was ready to turn north again — into Alaska!

The drive along Kluane Park and across the Yukon to the Alaska border at Beaver Creek was uneventful. The Alaska Highway had many frost heaves and breakups. I felt a certain travel weariness, and stopped and rested many a time. But a hearty welcome from my friends Dinah and Claus-M. Naske awaited me in Fairbanks, after that long and tiring journey.

Claus-M. wrote the text for my first Alaska book (Oxford University Press, 1985), and is Chairman of the History Department at the University of Alaska, Fairbanks. He had arranged a meeting the next day with the president of Frontier Flying Services Inc. We hoped to barter flying time on unsold seats for my photographs, an arrangement of benefit to both of us. Lynn Hajdukovich, the president's daughter, was responsible for the company's advertising and public relations. She was very enthusiastic.

The first flight chosen was to Kotzebue, on the tip of the Baldwin Peninsula, just north of the Arctic Circle on Kotzebue Sound and the Chukchi Sea,

Manufacturing Whale Oil, Pangnirtung, Baffin Island, N.W.T.,
August 1, 1929.

PHOTOGRAPH BY L.D. LIVINGSTONE — COURTESY OF THE NATIONAL ARCHIVES OF CANADA,
PA102682 — INDIAN AND NORTHERN AFFAIRS COLLECTION.

between Alaska and Siberia.

The mighty, meandering, ice-covered Yukon River dominated our view as our small twin-engined plane headed northwest from Fairbanks. But soon the rugged and wild Brooks Range appeared on our right, to the north, still in the grip of winter even though it was the first day of May and the sun was high in the sky. The Baldwin Peninsula lay below, a flat stretch of land meeting an endless expanse of frozen, snow-covered sea.

Approaching Kotzebue, we passed through a brownish-grey dustbowl that hung over a settlement surrounded by pristine whiteness. The brown dust was sand stirred up on the roads, covering everything with a layer of dust and sand. Wind gusts blew sharp grit in your face and made the skin burn.

A contact person soon delivered me to the most modern hotel in town. Situated right at the water's edge, this multi-storeyed grey wooden building contrasted sharply with many others in the village. It stood on pilings in the permafrost and around its perimeter was a series of steel coolers about six feet tall. They were all angled outward from the building to prevent the buildup of summer heat from thawing the permafrost and letting the building collapse, almost like the support pilings all along the above-ground sections of the Alaska oil pipeline. Inside it was warm and comfortable, even cozy. Big picture

windows overlooked the frozen sea. All the comforts imaginable: TV, radio, hot and cold running water. Yet, from the air, Kotzebue looked like a forlorn outpost in an endless white expanse. The logistics involved in moving all the building materials to a settlement in the extreme north are complicated and expensive. In the summer Kotzebue is a favourite destination of northern cruise ships coming up through the Bering Sea and Bering Strait for a brief glance at this outpost with its fabulous museum, its one tree, the "Kotzebue National Forest," and its Eskimo, Russian, and American history.

Here is manifest again the transition phase of a nomadic people caught between the attractions of a multi-faceted society and its wish to retain the traditional indigenous lifestyle.

The last point was driven home vividly during a meeting of the elders' council of the surrounding borough. It took place at the Kotzebue council office under the U.S. flag. I was allowed to sit in and take photographs. The main point on the agenda was an order of the State of Alaska and the government in Washington to close a home for the elderly and its attached medical facilities. It was noted by the authorities that a number of the elderly inmates had become very weak and ill soon after being admitted. The deteriorating health and the weight losses of the elderly pensioners and patients could not be ignored.

Food for all the inmates was prepared according to the nutrition guidelines set forth by federal and

Kingichamute Tom-Tom Players in ceremonial Customs.
Cape Prince of Wales, Alaska.

PHOTOGRAPH BY LOMEN BROTHERS, NOME. TAKEN 1901 — NATIONAL ARCHIVES OF CANADA,
7271809 — ALASKA AND POLAR REGIONS DEPT. UNIVERSITY OF ALASKA FAIRBANKS —
AL LOMEN COLLECTION.

region of the wild Brooks Range. Anaktuvuk Pass is both a geographical feature and an Inupiat settlement. Set on the continental divide, just west of Mt. Cocked Hat, at 7,610 feet the range's highest peak, it provides a spectacular view of the North Slope.

On the east side of Mt. Cocked Hat the Atigun Pass (4,752 feet) provides the break through the mountains for the Alaska oil pipeline from Prudhoe Bay to its seaside terminal at Valdez, on Prince William Sound. The Dalton Highway, a gravelled, all-weather supply road for Prudhoe Bay and the pipeline, winds its way along it. That road and the pipeline section running above ground were clearly visible from the windows of our twin-engined Dornier 228.

Lynn and I switched from side to side in the plane to view and photograph the glistening mountains in their white finery — peaks and valleys from horizon to horizon. A mere photograph could not come close to evoking the fleeting feelings of almost indescribable joy and awe that ran through us.

The plane cannot linger, as the eye and mind would like it to.

The final approach, through the peaks of Cocked Hat Mountain in the east and Castle Mountain in the west, was a vivid revelation of the reason for calling this area the "Gates of the Arctic."

After we drew up to the tiny wooden terminal, a number of cars and pick-up trucks literally surrounded us. Besides us, the passengers, our Dornier had cargo to unload.

state legislation. The traditional fare of the northern natives, the food that their metabolism was accustomed to, was strictly forbidden on the grounds that it was unhygienic! The white residential nutritionist confirmed the regulations. Despite the seriousness of the subject, there were laughs from the natives. As far as they were concerned, the facilities had to stay, and the nutrition had to be changed to their traditional "country food."

A decision was made to prepare the caribou, seal, and fish outside the sanitary residence kitchen and have it delivered to the elders every day. That resolution carried unanimously.

The community schools were holding spring festivals. There was laughter, friendly competition, and play everywhere, and food galore, both "country style" and white man's. I walked through the village in a bone-chilling wind that made photography difficult.

The extensive graveyard, now surrounded by multi-storeyed buildings, was crisscrossed by snowmobile tracks. Shortcuts for the living.

A couple of days later I got a chance to fly to the native settlements Allakaket and Bettles, in the southern foothills of the Brooks Range, just south and north of the Arctic Circle respectively. Then Lynn joined me for a flight into the "Gates of the Arctic" National Park, which straddles the highest

Through helpful contacts, we arranged for Gilbert Linccoln, a native elder, to take us caribou hunting. He knew where to find a small herd at that time of day. Gilbert's daughter Della came along with her video camera and Gilbert had his rifle slung over his chest. We were, of course, warmly dressed for the cold ride. I finally used my face mask for the first time. Sitting at the front of a sled behind a snowmobile, I expected snow to fly in my face, and it certainly did.

Deep into the mountains Gilbert spotted a herd of caribou slowly moving about. Even a careful approach alerted the animals to our presence, and they disappeared into a gully. Gilbert just smiled. "I know where they are heading. Let's move." He was right. We saw the caribou coming out of the gully, in single file, nice and slow. We dismounted and I got my long Apo-Telyt lens ready. It is heavy for hand-held shooting, but I got some good shots of this small group, with the mountain range looming blue in the background. We also spotted two hunters on another snowmobile ready to shoot. They spotted us through their binoculars and refrained from shooting, leaving the field to us.

Our attempt to get closer set the herd moving again to search for lichen under the snow on the lower mountain reaches. Then we heard the crack of a high-powered rifle. Gilbert did not like what he saw — an animal obviously hit in the leg. The stricken caribou tried to keep up with the disturbed herd but fell time and again, until it collapsed. Gilbert got very angry with the two white hunters from the village. He shouted to them to kill the caribou with a knife.

Then they closed in rapidly and fired the shot that ended the animal's life. We went over to them and found that they had started to skin their game. The hunter offered the animal to Gilbert, but he didn't need any meat, so it was distributed among people in the village. I took photographs of the butchering.

Warm from the excitement, I had taken off my thin face mask. As the machine flew across the snow, I protected my lens as well as I could from the steady barrage of snow and ice thrown up from the machine's rubber track. We were soon covered in white. The snowmobile was like a horse running for its stable, speeding faster as we left the mountains for the flatter terrain around the settlement. When the machine stopped in front of Gilbert's house, he looked at me, threw off his big skin mittens, and put two fingers of each hand on my cheeks. "Frostbite," he pronounced. His treatment was effective.

Their tea was delicious — soothing, hot, and sweet.

I had to leave my cameras and lenses outside, wrapped, as usual, in three layers of plastic bags, against certain condensation. I placed them in the cool entrance, between two doors.

A caribou leg was produced and placed on some tin in the middle of the floor of the modern kitchen. Out came the "ulu," the famous Eskimo women's knife. In Della's hands it was deftly used to cut some good-sized steaks from the hind leg. Onions were frying in the pan on the stove. What a smell! Since there were not enough dishes to serve the steaks, the ulu was used to cut cardboard into pieces of suitable size. They soaked up the excess fat nicely. Della got out her video gear and caught us stuffing ourselves. It was hilarious when Gilbert produced frozen "muktuk" from the fridge, some raw, some marinated. I tried it, and much to my surprise I actually liked the marinated version; I even had a second helping. Della put a raw piece between her teeth and cut it off with her ulu.

"Dessert, anyone?" Frozen blueberries, loads of them, with condensed milk. "More tea?" And I contributed a big chocolate bar. On their large TV we were soon able to see the hunt, the caribou slaughter, and our feast. It is hard to believe. There in the highest settlement in Alaska, where in the late nineteen-sixties there were only sod houses, we sat in a comfortable house watching a video of the afternoon's events, which we had all experienced. There were even some scenes of me chewing muktuk with a funny grin on my face. It seemed totally unreal.

A walk through the village followed. Caribou skins were hanging around many houses, some still stretched on frames. Dogs yelped at my legs. Alone, I stomped across the frozen snow to the outskirts and to higher ground. The wind had died down. Absolute stillness descended over mountains and valleys. Smoke rose from many a chimney in the distance, while twilight lingered.

Slowly I walked back to the village. Time to turn in. I was full of thoughts — the fantastic flight from Fairbanks in a very modern and quiet German-built Dornier DO 228, over the Yukon river and the foothills and across the Brooks Range; the descent between the mountains of the "Gates of the Arctic" into the Anaktuvuk Pass; and finally, all the friendly folk, both native and white. I felt very privileged.

As we headed back to the small airstrip to leave the next day, we met Gilbert Lincoln, grinning proudly, behind the steering wheel of a new blue Suzuki 4/4. A transport plane had delivered it that morning. No roads lead into or out of the village. Is this progress?

The open country of the Yukon Flats to the northeast of Fairbanks is Indian country. The Gwich'in settled there, close relatives of the people I met in Fort McPherson in the Canadian Northwest Territories and in Aklavik and Arctic Red River.

Fort Yukon, an older settlement at the confluence of the Porcupine, Sheenjek, Black, and Yukon rivers, feels different, in both its geography and its people, from Anaktuvuk Pass and the gigantic Brooks Range of mountains. Situated right on the Arctic Circle, it is river country, with myriads of bodies of water, flowing and stagnant. Its wide-open spaces and big skies are broken by black spruce, Arctic willows, muskeg, and soon by millions and millions of black flies and mosquitoes.

I was there on my own, although Lynn had arranged for me to meet Richard Caroll and his wife Kathy, both Gwich'in Indians. Kathy was a village administrator, and Richard a guide and beekeeper. We visited his hives, placed almost directly beneath the huge, abandoned radar towers of the DEW line. These monstrosities are remnants of the cold war.

It was a mild day. The remaining snow was soft and melting. The rivers showed signs of ridding themselves of winter's icy grip. Spring was in the air. Here I found the promise of long days without darkness.

In the settlement I also found an abandoned Hudson's Bay Company trading post, a resurrected fort with crumbling buildings and fences, and a battleground with several Christian denominations seeking to save the souls of the savages. Here too were graveyards. Divide and conquer is the white man's legacy.

Also evident was the devastating alcohol problem, which left people to wander in a state of stupor in a part of the village known as gun town. I had been warned not to take any photographs there.

Our northland is vast. It stretches from Greenland in the east to Alaska and Siberia in the west, encompassing different geographical regions, different climatic zones, and different human societies, which have evolved throughout centuries of adaptation. Despite all of their problems, frequently introduced by the white man, these societies that were mistreated and ignored are re-emerging to assert their vital indigenous identities.

They can teach Caucasians about the harmonies required for man's survival. They offer an alternative to the destructive mercantile thinking that has resulted in the massive consumption that threatens to destroy all our resources.

INTRODUCTION TO PITA AATAMI

Pita Aatami, President of Makivik Corporation of Kuujuak and Montreal is young, energetic, accomplished and smart. Makivik Corporation is the owner of Air Inuit and First Air, Canada's prime northern Airline and third largest in Canada. **HB**

NUNAVIK: TRANSFORMED IN MY LIFETIME

Pita Aatami

The contemporary Nunavik story has taken place in my lifetime. In November 2000 I turned 40. In March of that year I had won a renewed mandate as President of Makivik Corporation, the Nunavik equivalent of Premier.

My parents may have grown up in an igloo, but I lived in a small wooden house in Kuujjuaq, without hot and cold running water. My brothers and I did all the running for the water and wood. As children, we had hardly anything. We had our house, and the school. That was before the James Bay Agreement was signed. But we were never bored as children. We had sword fights, pretend wars, bicycle rides. We had no TV back then, so we had a lot of free time, which we put to good use. I've always been interested in what has been going on around me. In the early 1970s, when I was becoming a teenager, some significant developments were taking place in northern Quebec that would change our lives forever.

On 1970 Quebec's premier, Robert Bourassa, announced the creation of a massive hydro-electric project in the northern part of the province. Incredibly, the announcement of the project made no mention of the native peoples who lived in the region, who might be affected by the construction of the dams.

As I mentioned, we didn't have TV at the time, but we had radio and newspapers, and magazines would arrive regularly. Some of our leaders who were in their late teens, twenties, and thirties had gone to school in order to make themselves well understood in English.

Although I was very young, I can recall attending meetings that were held in Kuujjuaq in the years following Bourassa's announcement. The reaction among the Inuit was to fight the decision. We didn't want a mega-project to be built on our land without our consent. Our leaders created an organization called the Northern Quebec Inuit Association (NQIA) to make their voices heard as Inuit, and not together with the Indian Association of Quebec.

Bit by bit we made progress. Along with the Cree, we participated in a court case against Hydro-Québec to have the project stopped. We sent Inuit elders to the courthouse in Montreal to give testimony about our ancestral land use and hunting practices. It was incredible. It was as if we had to prove to outsiders that we had lived on our own land for thousands of years so that they wouldn't take it away from us, rip it up, build dams on it, flood it, make electricity with the dams, and, finally, not share the profits with us. We really thought Bourassa was crazy.

This was taking place at a time when feelings in Canada were just starting to shift for native peoples. Some of the buzzwords we take for granted today didn't exist. Even as simple an idea as "native rights," although it was becoming more familiar in legal circles, was not current among the population at large, and not in political circles. A January 1973 decision in western Canada known as the Calder case set an important precedent. The Nisga'a Indians sued for a declaration that they had aboriginal title. Although the case failed on procedural grounds, six of the seven judges recognized that aboriginal rights existed, and three of those six said the Nisga'a still had aboriginal rights.

So, on 15 November 1973, when we received word that we had won our court case against Hydro-Québec, we were elated. For us it was a major victory — a bit like David and Goliath. The result was that the government of Quebec announced four days later that they would negotiate a proper agreement with the Inuit and the Cree of northern Quebec regarding land rights. Still, though, they had in their minds that they were the ones who owned the land, not us.

To negotiate was a duty the Quebec government assumed when it acquired the land north of the fifty-fifth parallel in the 1912 Quebec Boundaries Extension Act. It had a duty to engage in treaty-making with the native peoples living in the region, to settle the land issue. It was a duty that had not been taken seriously until we took it to court over the James Bay Project.

So, we began to negotiate with Quebec. The Inuit, Cree, Quebec, Hydro-Québec, two of Hydro-Québec's development companies, and Canada sat down to negotiate the agreement. Much of the discussion dealt with the technical details of the construction of hydro-electric dams: there are diagrams of turbines in the James Bay Agreement. The issues of land rights and the creation of public institutions and of environmental and wildlife regimes came later in the talks. By 15 November 1974, we had settled on an Agreement in Principle.

Less than a year later, we had completed the negotiations and met the deadline of 11 November 1975. The James Bay and Northern Quebec Agreement (JBNQA) was signed in Quebec City at the midnight hour. A video of the signing ceremony — a rare slice of history — may be viewed on the Makivik Corporation web site.

The signing of the Agreement caused bitterness and dissent in our region. Families were ripped apart. It was as if we were giving up our Inuit nature. No one else in Canada has to do that when they sign a contract. Hydro-Québec went home after they signed the Agreement and went on building their dams. They were no longer going to be sued. As for us, the Inuit, we came back from the signing ceremony and were severely criticized by other native groups for "selling out" our land. We did obtain financial compensation from the Agreement, $90 million paid out over 20 years, the last payment of which was due in December 1996. We have received other payments related to the James Bay process since 1975 as well. These include $13 million from the Kuujjuamiut Agreement, signed in 1985. We also received $19.5 million in 1990 as part of the JBNQA Implementation Agreement. We obtained ownership of specific categories of land, and specific hunting and fishing rights.

Ironic as it may seem, after signing the Agreement we held formal title to what is known as Category One lands. These are managed by land-holding corporations. Our land is held collectively, which means we still could not own a plot of land and build a house. We can do that now, but we still don't own the land as individuals, we lease it for a long period of time.

We obtained an economic development corporation called Makivik Corporation. It is with Makivik Corporation that we were able to take the James Bay Agreement and implement it. Without Makivik, we surely would not have made all the advances we have made to this point.

There were transition years following the signing of the Agreement. The NQIA continued to operate, with an elected group of leaders. It expanded to include representation from all the communities in Nunavik. As I mentioned, not everyone accepted the signing of the Agreement. Three communities out of 15 did not support the work our leaders were doing. These were Puvirnituq (commonly spelled Povungnituk at the time), Ivujivik, and half the community of Salluit. As a result, these communities did not elect members to the Board of the Makivik Corporation in the early years. It took time, but the rifts healed, and now all the communities elect Board members.

Eventually, on 23 June 1978, Makivik Corporation formally came into being following the passage of an act in the National Assembly in Quebec City. Our executive members were elected by universal suffrage. We had six members on the executive (President, First Vice-President, Second Vice-President, Third Vice-President, Treasurer, and Secretary). We have since whittled this down to five (eliminating the position of First Vice-President). The Board has grown to 16, including members representing the Inuit who live in Chisasibi, Umiajaq (a new community built in the mid-1980s), and Killiniq (whose population was relocated all over Nunavik). In 1993 we appointed a six-member Board of Governors, whom we consider the elder statesmen of Nunavik, a body of sober second thought much like the Canadian Senate. With the passing of Governor Noah Qumaq in 1997 the Nunavik Governors are now five in number.

Having created this formal structure, we have established Makivik Corporation as an important political, economic, and social force in northern Quebec. In the Arctic, organizations such as Makivik are called "birthright corporations." This is because they have the exclusive mandate to represent the Inuit in their respective regions. Makivik Corporation was the first such organization, but all Inuit in Canada now have similar bodies working for them. In Labrador there is the Labrador Inuit Association. Nunavut Tungavik Incorporated (NTI) is the main organization for the Inuit of Nunavut. In the Western Arctic the Inuvialuit Regional Corporation manages the affairs of the Inuit of the Northwest Territories communities.

In the case of Nunavik, in northern Quebec, Makivik's mandate is vital to the development of the region. We've had to fight and struggle every step of the way to obtain what we have. The governments of Quebec and Canada are not providing services to our region because they are good guys. We very much have to spar with them politically to obtain the public goods that are due to us as citizens. And we are Canadian citizens.

I frequently point out that we live in municipalities in the province of Quebec, within Canada. We pay all provincial and federal taxes, and all income taxes. In fact, except for Chisasibi, the Inuit who live in the 14 Nunavik villages are among the highest taxed in Canada. Almost all consumer goods are sent up to the region by marine or air transport, because there is no road link to the Nunavik region. As a result, goods are taxed on the costs of transportation. We have worked tirelessly to demonstrate to governments in Quebec City and Ottawa that our region, which is essentially an island, is unfairly taxed. There are many places in Canada that benefit from transportation subsidies that reduce the cost of living in remote regions. The Magdalen Islands and Quebec's Lower North Shore are two examples. I'm pleased to say that despite the lengthy process involved in making these arguments, eventually governments are receptive, and I hope that similar programs will be implemented to ensure that there is fiscal fairness for the people who live in the Nunavik region.

We have Annual General Meetings, which are held each year in a different Nunavik community. In the early years, these meetings lasted close to two weeks, because they were preceded by a Board of Directors meeting. In addition to the Makivik Corporation directors and executives, we invited presidents of landholding corporations, all Nunavik mayors, and leaders of the major Nunavik organizations. During the course of the Annual Meetings we cover a wide range of topics. When Quebec held referendums in 1980 and 1995 on separating from Canada, we passed resolutions at our Annual meetings to create our own Inuit referendum, in addition to voting in the Quebec-wide referendum. In both cases Inuit voted massively in favour of remaining in Canada.

We have always invited ministers representing the governments of Canada and Quebec to our Annual Meetings, which take the form of an estates general. Because all of the Inuit leaders in Nunavik attend, these meetings provide an opportunity for a federal or provincial minister to address the Inuit public.

My approach has always been to work with people, as a group or as individuals, whether they are in government, business, or some other organization. I think that more progress is made this way than by engaging in lengthy conflicts to prove a point and force government or industry to the table. For example, in the early 1990s we learned that Falconbridge Limited wanted to develop a nickel mine at a site called Raglan. There used to be a mine there, but it had closed down. Falconbridge wanted to exploit the considerable nickel reserves there. Instead of throwing up roadblocks to the development project, we put on the hat of a developer. How could the project benefit the people in the closest communities, and the region as a whole? We entered into formal negotiations with Falconbridge, and in February 1995 signed the Raglan Agreement, which has proven to be a precedent-setting agreement in the Canadian mining industry.

We demonstrated to the Falconbridge officials that we had rights in the region, but also that we have business experience, and that we wanted to develop the project in partnership. We had specific long-term needs, especially the development of significant employment opportunities for our quickly growing young population. As well, we wanted to ensure that the project provided opportunities for the entrepreneurs among us to create their own small businesses independently, or in conjunction with other partners. We shared a business risk with Falconbridge, and emerged with a winning agreement that gives our region a boost. The experience we gained with Falconbridge provided a valuable lesson in the development process. We don't shy away from big projects.

As the millennium came to a close we still had unfinished business from the JBNQA. Even 25 years after its signing there were still parts of it that had not been fully implemented. A major project that had yet to be dealt with was the construction of proper marine facilities in all our communities.

During the 1980s and early 1990s we tackled the state of airport facilities in our villages, upgrading airstrips and terminal buildings. This was an immediate priority, considering the importance of air travel to and from our region. Work was also done during this period in upgrading the housing stock. But because we are a marine people, we had a pressing need for safer marine facilities. Some of our communities on Ungava Bay experience extremely high tides. We obtain much of our food from the sea. We're still hunters, catching seals, walrus, and whales. When we build breakwaters and clear floodplains of massive boulders, we improve our lives by extending the number of hunting hours, and increasing marine safety.

I have a particular fondness for this project, and a particular interest in how it has been going. We battled the federal government for years on the funding, and finally made a breakthrough in early

1998 to the tune of $30 million for the first phase. An additional $5 million was provided at our Annual General Meeting in March 2000 to accelerate the construction. What pleases me most, though, is that we are taking on the task of construction ourselves. We're buying the dump trucks, the rock crushers, and the graders. Most importantly, we are training local Inuit workers to use the heavy equipment to construct the breakwaters, clear the floodplains, and manage the projects locally. It makes a huge difference when we do it this way. The equipment will stay up north after the ten-year project is completed. We're completing one or two communities each summer, and the project is progressing well.

Similarly, we negotiated for two years with the government of Canada to prove that it had an obligation as a result of the James Bay Agreement for the provision of social housing for the Inuit of Nunavik. I must commend both the federal and provincial levels of government for demonstrating good faith during these talks. Despite the fact that an agreement had not been concluded, the two governments committed $10 million together in the spring of 1999 to ensure that the summer construction season of 1999 would not go by without new homes being built in the region. We built 46 homes and continued negotiating toward a Nunavik Social Housing Agreement by the spring of 2000. This agreement committed both levels of government to $10 million in funding per year for five years. The agreement is renewable after that time.

As with the Marine Infrastructure program, we took on the task of building the new houses ourselves. While we made some mistakes during the summer of 2000 with construction methods, we learned from the experience. The 60 new homes will be ready for their new occupants in March of 2001. We are eager to tackle the summer 2001 construction season.

In talking about these large development projects I wanted to give the sense that we are very consciously making efforts to ensure that the Inuit are benefiting from the development process. For example, it isn't enough just to get a development agreement with Falconbridge. The spirit of the agreement has to be such that the Inuit in our region play a part in the project. It's not enough just to get marine facilities in all our communities; I insist that Inuit learn how to operate the trucks and rock crushers, and take on skilled jobs on the sites. The same goes for the housing construction project. It was pleasing to read that over 65 percent of the workers on the housing construction project were Inuit.

A few final points will demonstrate how vital it is to settle sound and comprehensive land claims agreements. Despite its shortcomings, the JBNQA provided us with a pool of capital, which has been well invested in the stock, bond, and money markets, so that we have not only preserved our original capital, but more than doubled it. Furthermore, we have been able to create important regional companies, and to engage in joint ventures with other Inuit groups.

The first regional subsidiary company we created was Air Inuit, a regional airline that flies to each of the 14 Nunavik communities, and connects the Hudson's Bay coast with Montreal. More than 300 people work for Air Inuit.

Makivik Corporation purchased First Air in September 1990. In January 2000, 1,050 people worked at the airline. It is truly an Arctic airline, flying across the Canadian Arctic and to Greenland, and connecting the Arctic to southern Canada. It is Canada's third largest airline. I am the chairman.

Our joint venture activities include a company called Pan Arctic Inuit Logistics (PAIL), which operates and maintains unmanned radar stations for the Canadian military. PAIL is owned jointly with Inuit in Labrador, Nunavut, and the Western Arctic. We are in the marine transport business as well. In 1999 we entered into a partnership agreement with the Inuit of Nunavut to manage a company called Nunavut Eastern Arctic Shipping (NEAS), which provides marine shipping services to communities in the Easter Arctic.

Looking back on the changes that have taken place in Nunavik over my short lifetime I am amazed at the transformation — from the stone age to the computer age. We have made considerable progress, and we have numerous challenges ahead of us. Essentially, we have the challenge of ensuring that our people take advantage of the numerous resources available to them for the creation of new enterprises, new products, and new processes. Makivik is always here to help.

nakurmiik

Pita Aatami
— President, Makivik Corporation

INTRODUCTION TO PAUL QUASSA

Paul Quassa was the President and long time leader and negotiator for the NTI (Nunavut Tungavik Incorporated), which is the trustee for all Inuit of Nunavut and the guardian of the Land Claim Settlement for Nunavut. As this essay shows, Paul is a diverse, eloquent and intelligent Inuk. **HB**

LOOKING AHEAD

Paul Quassa

It is now just over seven and a half years since we Inuit signed a Comprehensive Land Claims Agreement with the Crown. We have seen various events follow, according to the purpose of the Land Claims Agreement, the major one being the reality of the Inuit dream of governing themselves, on their own terms, while remaining part of the Confederation of Canada. We have also seen the creation of a government, and the creation of a new territory, the Nunavut Settlement Area.

We have seen an enormous shift to the Inuit — who are 85 percent of the population of Nunavut — taking control of major infrastructure within Nunavut Territory and of the major means of transportation in Nunavut; working with major mineral development agencies and being paid for these activities; being the major offshore resource gatherers and doing it commercially; and the list goes on.

That has happened within eight years, and this tells me that land claims agreements can work for you if you implement them to your full capacity, although you also need to ensure that the other parties meet their obligations.

The Mission Statement of Nunavut Tunngavik Incorporated (NTI) refers very clearly to the "Economic, Social and Cultural Well-Being of Inuit Through the Implementation of the Nunavut Land Claims Agreement." With such direction, NTI has established programs such as income support programs for beneficiaries, Elders, and Hunters, and scholarships for Inuit youth, who make up over 50 percent of the population of Nunavut.

We also have a Nunavut Implementation Training Commission, which focusses on training Inuit to get into the Nunavut government workforce. It is an obligation of Nunavut government to ensure that a representative proportion of government employees be Inuit.

NTI is now considering delivering more benefits to its beneficiaries. Most of the benefits would be indirect, and would be at the community level. There are 27 communities within the Nunavut Settlement Area.

We are also talking about direct monetary benefits.

Nunavut beneficiaries now number about 25,000, and are scattered in our 27 municipalities. Inuit, through the Land Claims Agreement, are the largest private landholders in North America, and are now making use of their lands. Inuit have the right of first refusal in developing tourist sports lodges, and are sole owners of soapstone throughout the Nunavut Settlement Area.

We are members of all the Institutions of Public Government (IPGs), which make decisions concerning developments within the Land Claim area, including the management of wildlife and water.

This is where we are now in Nunavut. The projects and activities that I have mentioned are just a few of those we are examining and still working on.

We want to see the Inuit become self-sufficient and self-reliant.

This is what our Land Claims Agreement was meant to be, and if we implement the Agreement to our best abilities, it will do its work. I believe Inuit now have the confidence to show the rest of the country that they can manage and run their own affairs as they had in the past as independent people in their own homeland.

Certainly all the work is not done yet, for the Land Claims Agreement is a living agreement. It will keep moving, and it will keep growing, and it will forever work toward the full self-reliance and self-sufficiency of the Inuit. It is also imperative that governments live up to their obligations according to the Land Claims Agreement. I believe that Inuit in the future will utilize and develop Inuit lands, and that Inuit will have a stronger sense of their identity and recognize their distinctiveness among the rest of Canadians.

Inuit in Nunavut can and will be an inspiration to people around the world. They have demonstrated that numbers don't necessarily count, if the people have vision and willpower. A population of approximately 23,000 was able to change the map of a country. That was willpower.

Inuit are recognized as the major players and are feeling more at home in their own land after almost a hundred years. The coming hundred years will see Inuit becoming one of the major players in the world. They have learned much, and there is much they want to do. It will better the lives not only of Inuit, but of all who listen to and work with them.

We have survived the harshest climate in the world and we have shown that we can survive incidents of displacement. Inuit have been consistent and persistent in what they do, and will continue to be so.

There has been a move to connect with other Inuit throughout the circumpolar world and our energies and activities are expanding through this area. Inuit of the circumpolar world have much in common. There are many opportunities out there; we will keep our eyes on the vision. We now have the resources.

INTRODUCTION TO NELLIE COURNOYEA

Nellie Cournoyea, soft spoken, yet fiery if necessary, has held many pivotal roles in the struggle of her northern people to regain control over their lives and destinies. She was Premier of the Northwest Territories before the establishment of Nunavut, perhaps the major accomplishment during her tenure. Inuit, Indians and white people alike respected her in that position of stewartship for all the northern people. **HB**

BACKGROUND TO THE INUVIALUIT FINAL AGREEMENT

Nellie Cournoyea

Prior to the settling of comprehensive claims in Northern Canada, claims were established on the U.S. side of the border, in Alaska. These were very different from those eventually settled in Canada, and are a useful demonstration of the varying oppositions of negotiating governments, and the defining and eventual granting of aboriginal rights.

In 1867, the United States bought Alaska from Russia for $7.2 million. The Tlingit protested the sale in 1867. With the discovery of gold in Alaska in 1898, the Gold Rush was on. In addition, fishing, trapping, sealing, and logging attracted settlers to the "Last Frontier."

In 1935, the Tlingit and Haida sued to establish their aboriginal claim to lands taken for the development of the Tongass National Forest. The judgment made in 1959 said that they were entitled to compensation and ruled that the purchase of 1867 did not extinguish their aboriginal title. In 1968, the Tlingit and Haida were awarded $7.5 million.

In 1958, Alaska became a state. The Statehood Act disclaimed any right to land or property held by natives or in trust for them. Under the Act, the State had the right to select 103 million acres. In addition, the State tried to regulate native harvesting, which led to major friction with Alaska's aboriginal peoples.

By 1966, the Alaska Federation of Natives was formed. It called for the freeing of all dispositions of federal lands until land claims could be settled; it called on Congress to pass a land claim settlement bill.

In 1968, oil was discovered in Prudhoe Bay. The oil companies and legislators (both State and Federal) agreed that a land claim should be settled with the Inupiat of the North Slope.

In 1971, the Alaska Native Comprehensive Settlement Act (ANCSA) was passed by Congress. "Negotiations" were conducted in the usual manner of bill drafting in the United States — not in a negotiating forum that Canadians are used to.

Canadian claims guaranteed beneficiaries access to local wildlife through exclusive and preferential harvesting rights on a species basis; the U.S. claim offered the same use of resources to beneficiaries and non-beneficiaries alike, with the notable exception of certain marine mammal species.

The Alaskan Act was based on a very conscious and articulated philosophy of integrating Alaskan natives into mainstream America. It recognized the paramount need for economic development and financial self-reliance. The Act extinguished all aboriginal claims, including land title and hunting rights. Finally, the Act provided a cash settlement of $12,000 to each shareholder.

There were three eligibility criteria for enrolment as a beneficiary: one-quarter Alaskan native blood, a birthdate before 18 December 1971, and U.S. citizenship. There was a 20-year moratorium on the sale or transfer of shares to non-natives. No government funding was provided for the Inupiat to pursue the Settlement. Money was raised through a variety of community means. Some independent analysis of the settlement produced during the 1980s indicated that the Alaskan claim was an overall failure, by any measure.

The Inuvialuit Final Agreement (IFA) is based on the Canadian principles for the settlement of land claims; that is, traditional land use and occupancy and the acceptance of the principle of self-determination for aboriginal people. The Alaskan claim is based on the principles of equality expressed in the U.S. Constitution, and the need under the Constitution to integrate Alaskan natives into mainstream America.

The Alaskan claim does not recognize harvesting rights, unlike the IFA, in which harvesting rights for Inuvialuit are recognized as a part of aboriginal rights within Canada.

In addition, the Alaskan claim does not recognize land title in the same way that it is recognized in the IFA. In Canada, aboriginal title to the land is permanent and cannot be limited by time or transferred to anyone other than the Crown.

The Alaskan claim was particularly interesting to the Inuvaluit negotiators of the IFA from the perspective of avoiding the pitfalls inherent in the Alaskan claim.

The IFA created two principal management structures: the Inuvialuit Game Council (IGC) and the Inuvialuit Regional Corporation (IRC). The IGC is the body primarily concerned with renewable resources management. It is composed of a chairman and at least one representative from the Inuvialuit Hunters and Trappers Committees (HTCs) of Aklavik, Inuvik, Tuktoyaktuk, Paulatuk, Sachs Harbour, and Holman Island. Its purpose is to "represent the collective Inuvialuit interest in wildlife," with one of its most important functions being the appointment of Inuvialuit members to all joint government/Inuvialuit bodies having an interest in wildlife. The IFA does not spell out the relationship between the IGC and the IRC explicitly, but it seems almost deliberately to have given these two bodies fundamentally opposed mandates: conservation on the one hand, and economic development on the other. During the negotiations, the

Inuvialuit saw the inherent conflict in having the same organization responsible for development and for renewable resources management. The need to avoid this conflict extends right down to the community level. It is impossible for an Inuvialuk to represent the interests of his or her community fully and impartially with respect to either management or development. Those asked to do so are placed in a conflict of interest, and experience tense relations with their neighbours. Such conflict and tension are anathema to Inuit culture. A strong land ethic, and the need for harmony in the community, were the driving forces behind the creation of the IGC.

It is interesting to note that in March 1997 the Government of the Northwest Territories (GNWT) amalgamated the department responsible for wildlife management with that responsible for development (Economic Development and Tourism and Energy Mines and Petroleum Resources). All other governments in Canada keep their departments of wildlife management and development separate for the same reasons as the Inuvialuit. The only exception to this is the federal Department of Indian Affairs and Northern Development (DIAND), in which the ongoing stress created by the conflict between the two mandates has caused, and continues to cause, internal rearrangements. Only time will tell if the GNWT will have any better success.

Part of the task of resolving the relationship between the conservation mandate and the development mandate falls to the various co-management bodies created under the IFA, collectively referred to as the Renewable Resources Committees. There are five of them: a Wildlife Management Advisory Council for the Northwest Territories and another for the North Slope of the Yukon; the Fisheries Joint Management Committee; the

Environmental Impact Screening Committee; and the Environmental Impact Review Board. Representation on each of these bodies is half Inuvialuit (IGC-appointed) and half government-appointed, with a chairman appointed by the government, with Inuvialuit approval. The chairman of the Fisheries Joint Management Committee is appointed directly by the Committee members.

The wildlife Management Advisory Councils have broad authority, encompassing wildlife and habitat management, setting of quotas, and policy and legislative review.

The IFA contains all of the required ingredients for a co-management regime. It recognizes preferential or exclusive harvesting rights, control of access to the resources, participation in management, relevance of traditional knowledge, and modern scientific approaches to conservation.

Today the co-management regime in the Settlement Region works very well. However, in 1986 the Inuvialuit decided to break away from the position of the Inuit Circumpolar Conference (ICC), which opposed the shipping of oil and gas by tanker, and to consent to such shipment by Gulf Canada from the Beaufort Sea, with no provision for environmental assessment and review. This decision, which was made before the co-management institutions and procedures were fully established, did not augur well for environmental concerns.

In 1990, Gulf proposed a three-year program to drill a series of wells in the transition zone between the permanent pack ice and the land-fast ice — this was referred to as the Kulluk Drilling Program. The Environmental Impact Review Board (EIRB) turned the proposal down, because Gulf and the federal government had not prepared for a major oil well blowout in the Beaufort Sea, nor had they spelled out Gulf's liability should a disaster occur.

First Nations negotiators want the co-management agreement to be treaty-like, recognizing and affirming treaty and aboriginal rights on the basis of the Constitution Act of 1982 and using the guidelines of the Sparrow ruling. Co-management is to be based on the principles of conservation and sustainable development, and there has to be an effective integration of the "two bodies of wisdom."

INTRODUCTION TO CLAUS-M. NASKE

Claus-M. Naske, German born Chairman of the History Department, University of Alaska, Fairbanks, is also President of University of Alaska Press. A well-known authority on arctic history, Alaska's and Canada's, he is the author of many books and papers, as well as a keen traveller and canoeist. **HB**

THE MODERNIZATION OF ALASKA

Claus-M. Naske

In 1701, V.V. Atlasov, the Russian military commander at Anadyrsk on the Chukotsk Peninsula, wrote that various native Chukchi who lived on East Cape and at the mouth of the Anadyr River reported that "opposite this impassible cape is [an] island, and from this island [mainland Alaska at Cape Prince of Wales] when [the] sea is frozen arrive foreigners [Kinugmiut Eskimos], speaking their own language."

In response to the Chukchi natives' unwillingness to submit to Russian rule, in 1711 authorities sent out Peter Popov from Anadyrsk Ostrog with a small group of Cossacks to observe them. Besides his observations about the Chukchi and their land and resources, he wrote the following about the Strait of Anian and the Big Land beyond: "There are big-toothed people on that island, and their beliefs and other customs and language are distinctive and not Chukchi, and for a long time there has been no peace between the cape Chukchis and these islanders." They saw ten of these islanders who had been taken prisoner by the Chukchi: "The [big] teeth of these people, except their natural teeth, are small walrus tusks that are put in their cheeks alongside their natural teeth." In the summer they crossed from that cape to that island in kayaks in one day, and in the winter in one day on reindeer, without baggage. Popov reported that the island contained "sable, martens, every sort of fox including Arctic fox, wolves, wolverines, polar bears, and sea otters; and they keep great herds of reindeer. The islanders lived just like the Chukchi, and they have no chieftains."

These denizens of the far north have fascinated explorers for several hundred years. What has accounted for this, in part, was their living in a land where it is nearly always cold, subsisting on a predominantly meat diet, and for some, in the eastern Arctic, building houses from snow. They hunted great whales from frail skin-covered boats, and polar bears with spears. Some ate fish as a steady diet and never saw a bowhead whale or polar bear. Much of the literature portrayed them as occupying a barren, icebound coast, but some lived on the edges of coastal forests and some so far inland that they never saw the sea. Also, some Eskimos never used dog teams, or hunted seals at their breathing holes.

Although most explorers did not stress it, their technology was superb and their varied means for taking game unmatched by other aboriginal hunters. Above all, they often developed unique survival techniques. Their remoteness in the Arctic, the inaccessibility of their homeland, and its lack of economic importance until fairly recently meant that Western intrusions were seldom extensive. All of these factors contributed to their survival.

In the earliest accounts, Alaskan Eskimos are characterized as distinct from other Eskimos. Unlike most of their Canadian kinfolk, they did not base their livelihood on hunting seals at breathing holes, nor did they build snow houses. They did not concentrate on open-water sealing as the East Greenlanders did or emphasize hunting on the sea ice as did the Polar Eskimos. The Alaskan Eskimos were much more diversified, as were those of West Greenland and Labrador. Also, the Alaskan Eskimos often had secular leaders; in many cases their social festivities were elaborate; and some groups, as anthropologist Ernest S. Burch, Jr., has written, possessed a clear sense of common identity. At established market centres people came together for trading. Shamans, inuas, and trances represented the essence of Eskimo religion. These people often held complex annual ceremonies in which the whole village participated and great wealth might be redistributed. Travellers reported masked dancers, and some writers speculated that the Alaskan Eskimos had borrowed some of their cultural activities from the northeastern Siberian peoples. Alaskan Eskimos also had cultural ties to the east, holding in common with Mackenzie and northern Alaskan Eskimos such things as men's houses, driftwood structures, fish netting, yearly ceremonies, and secular leaders.

Some English explorers reached northern Alaska by ship from the east, and others arrived from the west. John Franklin explored westward from the Mackenzie in 1826, but, encountering hostile Mackenzie Eskimos, Franklin travelled as fast as possible; he did not seek out Alaskan Eskimos and had few contacts with them. In 1826 Frederick W. Beechey cruised north of Bering Strait. Franklin and Beechey were to rendezvous at Kotzebue Sound, but when the former failed to appear, the *Blossom* sailed northward beyond Icy Cape. Thomas Elson, commanding a barge from the *Blossom*, sailed farther east and became the first European to reach Point Barrow.

Franklin had boated as far as the Return Islands, which left an unmapped area of about 250 miles between those islands and Point Barrow. The Hudson's Bay Company sent Thomas Simpson and Peter W. Dease in 1837 to map the gap. The party reached Point Barrow but remained only a short time. The travellers reported that the Barrow people craved tobacco, which they chewed and smoked. Tobacco smoking had originated among American Indians, and the Portuguese introduced it to Europe in 1558. It was widely grown in Europe by 1600, and the Russians soon carried it across Siberia. The Chukchi and Siberian Eskimos traded Russian tobacco into Alaska before the arrival of the Europeans. At the time of contact with Europeans, all Alaskan Eskimos apparently smoked, and the practice had spread east to the Mackenzie Eskimos.

Anthropologists estimate the Alaska Eskimo population to be roughly 29,000, almost three times that of Canadian Eskimos. Eskimo culture was also most diversified in Alaska. A linguistic boundary delimited two major Eskimo groups in Alaska. Those living north of Norton Sound, the Inuit, spoke Inupiaq. To the south lived the Yuit, who spoke Yupik. Inupiaq speakers and Yupik speakers were unintelligible to each other.

In 1848 few European ships had sailed the Alaska coast north of Bering Strait. In that year, new whaling grounds were discovered in the Arctic Ocean. The whaling barque *Superior*, of Sag Harbor, New York, was the first American vessel to pass through Bering Strait into the Arctic Ocean. The barque took so many whales that the next year 154 whalers cruised north of Bering Strait, and by 1854 the first whalers sailed east of Point Barrow.

Whalers were not interested in Eskimo customs, but their rapacious exploitation of the bowhead whale eventually adversely affected the Eskimos' livelihood. John Simpson, the surgeon aboard the *Plover* throughout its six Arctic winterings, authored the first detailed report about the northern Alaskan Eskimos. The ship wintered in a Siberian harbour, then along the western Seward Peninsula, and eventually, from 1852 to 1854, at Point Barrow.

During the First International Polar Year, in 1881, Lieutenant Patrick H. Ray of the U.S. Army Eighth Infantry commanded an expedition by a military party to which John Murdoch, a sergeant in the U.S. Army Signal Corps, a naturalist with an M.A. degree from Harvard University, was attached.

His studies from 1881 to 1883 resulted in a major monograph about the Barrow Eskimos.

In 1867, the United States purchased Alaska from Russia. Traders and whalers were the most dispersed and visible groups of outsiders. By 1880, the Revenue Marine Service Revenue Cutter *Corwin* sailed in northern waters, and the Secretary of the Treasury wrote that "to thousands of half-civilized natives she represents the majesty and power of the nation, and dispenses such justice as humanity and the needs of the people call for."

Eventually, missionaries, schoolteachers, nurses, physicians, construction workers, and various government and military personnel followed. They all contributed to the Eskimos' growing awareness of western society and culture and contributed to major cultural changes.

After the Second World War, the steadily increasing contacts with Caucasians persuaded many Eskimos to adopt some of the material and social traits of western society. By the 1930s they were abandoning their traditional partially underground dwellings in ever greater numbers and constructing multi-room frame houses. They bought western goods and services and started to wear western clothing. They also participated in western religious and secular holidays. Concurrently, interest in traditional activities such as hunting and fishing, games, dances, and skilled crafts declined and in some instances disappeared altogether. In short, the Eskimos identified more and more with western cultural patterns and, in the process, discarded much of their cultural heritage; eventually much of the lifestyle of the Eskimo was destroyed.

Anthropologist Norman A. Chance has written that, unlike many Caucasians who broadened their opportunities with the industrialization of the United States, Eskimos, Indians, and members of some other minority groups found themselves limited by geographical and social isolation, lack of educational and occupational skills, racism, and economic exploitation, as well as by social behaviour and cultural beliefs of their own that were not very effective when applied to life in a quickly changing industrialized society. Chance then pointed out that the long history of exploitation and misery stemmed from early Eskimo-white contacts, including those with Russian fur traders and whalers, who left their mark in northern coastal villages, where the Eskimos were already reduced by European diseases and alcohol-related disorders.

The various religious denominations viewed the Eskimos as uncivilized heathens, and worked to convert them to the "superior ways" of the western world. In addition, the federal government and teachers, as well as missionaries, supported by federal statutes, attempted to assimilate the Eskimos as quickly as possible. But even when the Eskimos accepted Christianity, the Caucasians still relegated them to an inferior status, operating according to the commonly accepted myth of social Darwinism, which explained Caucasian superiority in technological, social, and cultural spheres as being a result of their natural superiority.

The federal government failed to assimilate the Eskimos and Indians rapidly, but it nevertheless continued its assimilationist policies. As more Caucasians, drawn by the gold rushes, came to Alaska, federal legislation extended the homestead laws, established a legal system, and created the rudiments of a civil government, but failed to designate or protect native landholdings. The original policy of integrated schools ended in 1905, when the federal government assumed responsibility for the education of all native children in Alaska. These schools provided an inferior education for the natives, which neither developed their traditional skills nor prepared them to qualify for vocational or professional training.

Alaska's resources continued to be utilized more intensively, but Eskimos participated only marginally in these developments. Whalers often employed them, as did the commercial salmon fishing industry in Bristol Bay. Favourable fur prices from the early 1900s until the beginning of the Great Depression in 1929 also offered some opportunities for cash income, but Eskimos had no secure economic base other than that derived from their traditional subsistence activities.

The Second World War and its aftermath revolutionized Alaska. Military personnel and their dependents, together with large numbers of postwar settlers, including many professionals, soon outnumbered Alaska's native population. With the onset of the Cold War, Alaska's economy shifted from resource extraction to military spending, which financed defence facilities and transportation. Education expanded, as did the health and service industries, providing increased job opportunities for native and white Alaskans. But booms were followed by busts, when government spending declined and unemployment increased. The Eskimos who moved from their villages to the new construction centres suffered especially during the bust periods, because they were the last to be hired and the first to be laid off. Yet they were receiving better health care than before, educational opportunities continued to expand, and geographical mobility helped to expand their knowledge of white Alaska and the larger world beyond.

Congress admitted Alaska as the forty-ninth state in 1959, and statehood, together with the civil rights movement in the contiguous states, created a new consciousness about minorities and their rights as citizens. The new state government began to incorporate Eskimo and Indian schools into the state system. High school attendance became easier with the construction of regional and, eventually, village schools, and university scholarships benefited those who were qualified.

In the early 1960s the levelling-off and then decline of defence spending led to unemployment. The federal and state governments intervened and made efforts to improve the economic and social conditions of Alaska's natives. Area economic development programs, the expansion of manpower training, the construction of health-care facilities, and community-action projects were elements of President Lyndon B. Johnson's "Great Society" programs. Yet in 1968, the U.S. Federal Field Committee for Development Planning in Alaska concluded that low income and living standards for most Alaska natives and their almost total lack of opportunity contrasted sharply with the high incomes, moderate living standards, and reasonable opportunities for most white Alaskans.

The fact that most of Alaska's Eskimos continued to live in villages far removed from areas of economic development accounted, in part, for their poor conditions. But Eskimos who migrated to the urban centres of south-central and interior Alaska did not experience greatly improved economic and social conditions. In short, it became clear that in order to fit the occupational needs of Alaska's rapidly modernizing economy, the natives needed at least the equivalent of a high-school education.

By 1970 increasing numbers of white and native Alaskans had recognized that educational programs needed to be expanded and significantly improved if natives were to be given an opportunity to compete in Alaska's labour market. With a view to improving the quality of existing schools, the personnel of schools operated by the Bureau of Indian Affairs

and by the state became more and more supportive new teacher preparation programs and in the introduction of bicultural and bilingual materials in the predominantly native schools. This approach was countered, however, by the continued insistence that natives become like whites, on the assumption that white middle-class values and institutions are superior to those of native Americans. In short, the schools largely failed to prepare students for full participation in Alaska's economic and social structure.

What natives needed in order to participate fully in Alaska's economy and its social and political life was political organization. The event that set into motion the political development of Alaska's natives was the territory's admission as the forty-ninth state in 1959. The statehood act allowed Alaska 25 years to select approximately 103.5 million acres from the vacant, unappropriated public domain. Since Congress had never conclusively determined the status of native land rights, this act threatened the expropriation of claimed lands, countering the Organic Act of 1884, which stated that natives should not be disturbed in the use or occupancy of their land, and that Congress would determine their land claims.

The new state proceeded cautiously with its selections. In the meantime, Alaska's natives, who constituted about one-fifth of the state's population in 1960, continued to live mostly where they constituted a majority, namely in the approximately 200 villages and settlements widely scattered across rural Alaska. They confidently expected to continue using the land as their ancestors had done for thousands of years.

Soon, however, threats to native land rights emerged, to which the natives responded by forming local and regional organizations, and in October

1966 eight regional native associations, formed to protect land rights, combined to establish the Alaska Federation of Natives (AFN), a statewide organization. The fear of losing the lands they had claimed radicalized the natives, and between 1960 and 1968 the inhabitants of the most remote settlements came to understand what was at stake. Of major importance in the final solution to the native land claims was the 1968 announcement of the major Prudhoe Bay petroleum discovery, and the subsequent North Slope oil rush.

Actually, the first threat to native lands had occurred as early as 1957, when the Atomic Energy Commission (AEC) established the Plowshare Program for the use of atomic energy for peaceful purposes. By the end of the year the agency had designed "Project Chariot," a massive explosion equal to 2.4 million tons of TNT. Physicists decided to excavate an artificial harbour at Cape Thompson on Alaska's northwest coast. The agency authorized some studies, and then decided to schedule the blast for 1960. The village council of Point Hope, located near the proposed blast site, voted unanimously to oppose the experiment. In 1961, the village Health Council appealed directly to President John F. Kennedy to stop the proposed blast. In Point Barrow, another controversy, this one concerning hunting rights, developed, and in November 1961 representatives from all along the coast met in that northernmost village for a conference on native rights. It was sponsored by the Association on American Indian Affairs, a private charitable organization based in New York City. Eskimo and public opposition eventually forced the federal government to abandon "Project Chariot." The Point Barrow conference also resulted in the formation of the first regional native organization since the founding of the Alaska Native Brotherhood in southeast Alaska nearly half a century earlier. It adopted the name Inupiat Paitot, the People's Heritage.

The next threat developed in 1961, when the state wanted to create a recreation area near the Athapaskan village of Minto. The state wanted to construct a road into the area to make it accessible to residents of Fairbanks, with an eye also on the future development of oil and other resources in the area. Minto residents protested and asked the Department of the Interior to protect their rights. Interior responded late in 1961, filing protests on behalf of Minto and three other villages concerning 5.8 million acres and conflicting with 1.7 million acres of state selection.

Between 1962 and 1966 threats to native claimed lands multiplied, and the Minto story was repeated over and over again. The most spectacular threat involved the proposal to build a dam 530 feet high and 4,700 feet long at the Rampart Canyon on the Yukon River at a cost of several billion dollars. The dam was to generate 5 million kilowatts of electricity but would put under several hundred feet of water the entire Yukon Flats, a vast network of sloughs, marshes, and potholes that is one of the largest wildfowl breeding grounds in North America. Native protests as well as public opposition and agency resistance eventually killed the plan.

During these controversies the state had continued to select and claim its land grant. The only recourse open to natives was to file protests to state land selections, so that between 1961 and 1968 their protest filings covered almost 337 million acres out of Alaska's total acreage of 375 million acres. Finally, in 1966, Secretary of the Interior Stewart L. Udall ordered a land freeze until Congress could sort out the various claims. This, of course, impeded state land selections.

In 1968, Atlantic-Richfield announced the discovery of oil on Alaska's North Slope. By 1969 the parameters of the gigantic 9.6 billion barrel Prudhoe Bay oilfield were known. In the fall of 1969 the state held its twenty-third competitive oil and gas lease sale in Anchorage. Since statehood Alaska had held a total of twenty-two lease sales, which had netted less than $100 million. Then in one day the state sold oil leases on less than .001 percent of its total land mass and raised more than $900 million. Euphoria reigned, but it soon became apparent that unless native claims were settled, no oil would reach tidewater at Valdez via the proposed 800-mile pipeline from Prudhoe Bay, since the line, in part, crossed native-claimed land.

After much manoeuvring by the various interest groups, Congress passed the precedent-setting Alaska Native Claims Settlement Act (ANCSA) of 1971, and President Richard M. Nixon signed it into law. In essence, it conveyed to Alaska's natives approximately 44 million acres of land in fee simple title and to nonprofit corporations title to the surface estate in the lands conveyed to the villages. The Act also directed that twelve regional corporations be organized to assume title to subsurface estate in the lands conveyed to the villages and full title to the additional acreage divided among them on a population basis. The U.S. Treasury was to pay $462.5 million over an eleven-year period, while the remaining $500 million was to come from a 2 percent royalty on production and another 2 percent on bonuses and rentals from land in Alaska thereafter conveyed under the Statehood Act. It excluded Naval Petroleum Reserve No. 4. Each regional corporation also had to divide among all 12 entities 70 percent of the mineral revenues it received.

Each regional corporation also had the responsibility of distributing among the village corporations in the region no less than 50 percent of its share of the $962.5 million monetary awards, as well as 50 percent of all revenues derived from sub-surface resources. This provision, however, did not apply to revenues received by the regional corporations from profits from their business ventures. Furthermore, for the first five years after the act became law, 10 percent of the revenues from the first two sources mentioned above were to be distributed among the native stockholders of the corporation.

The act also enabled natives who had moved out of state to organize a thirteenth regional corporation if they so desired, rather than receive stock in one of the twelve regional corporations. This thirteenth corporation would receive its pro rata share of the $962.5 million monetary award, but no land, and would not share in the mineral revenues of the other regional corporations.

The act also explicitly extinguished all claims the natives may have had based on aboriginal use and occupancy of lands and adjacent waters, including aboriginal hunting and fishing rights, but it also stated that none of its provisions "shall replace or diminish any right, privilege, or obligation of the United States or the State of Alaska to protect and promote the rights and welfare of natives as citizens of the United States or of Alaska."

Soon dissatisfaction with the terms of the ANCSA developed among many members of the Native community. There were numerous aspects of the settlement that disturbed villagers in rural Alaska, particularly the abolition of all native claims in exchange for the settlement, and especially claims to hunting and fishing rights that guaranteed the continuation of their subsistence lifestyle. By 1980 Alaska natives, politically much more sophisticated than a decade before, determined to reverse the ANCSA's extinguishment of their hunting and fishing rights. They accomplished this by trading their support for the Alaska National Interest Lands Conservation Act (ANILCA), a massive land withdrawal and classification proposal that finished the division of Alaska that had begun in the Alaska Statehood Act of 1958, for environmentalist support for ANILCA's Title VIII subsistence provisions. This provision, in a sense, multiplied the extinguishment of native hunting and fishing claims in ANCSA. But unlike previous such settlements, the ANILCA did not grant Alaska natives off-reservation or other exclusive rights to hunt or fish because of their membership in a particular tribe. Instead, recognizing political realities, the ANILCA created subsistence protection for most rural Alaskan residents, native and non-native alike.

After the enactment of ANILCA in 1980, natives turned to other objectionable provisions of the ANCSA, such as the corporate form of organization, the enrolment of natives born after 18 December 1971 (the date when President Richard M. Nixon signed the Act into law), the threat that lands not developed by 1991 might be taxed and eventually lost, and the provision that corporate shares were to become negotiable in 1991, which posed the threat of takeovers of the corporations by non-natives.

Responding to these issues, the Inuit Circumpolar Conference, an international organization of Eskimos from Alaska, Canada, and Greenland, appointed Canadian jurist Thomas R. Berger to conduct the Alaska Native Review Commission to examine the impact of the ANCSA. The World Council of Indigenous Peoples, an international organization of native peoples, co-sponsored the work of the commission.

Berger travelled to native villages all over Alaska to listen to the concerns of the population. He compiled an enormous hearing record, and then summarized his findings and recommendations in a volume entitled *Village Journey*.

Berger summarized the Act, its promises, and what he called its unravelling. He then explained that "United States policy toward Native Americans has always incorporated two contradictory ideas." The first led to efforts to assimilate native Americans through the adoption of measures designed to systematically undermine the "integrity of the Indian tribes." The division of Indian land into individually owned parcels exemplified this policy, as did the ANCSA. The other tendency had been the "explicit recognition of the fact that native government has a distinct place under the Constitution, together with the affirmation of communal land tenure." Berger pointed out that Chief Justice John Marshall "powerfully articulated this policy during the nineteenth century, and both Congress and the executive branch had espoused it from time to time since then." In Alaska, however, this had never been explicitly agreed to.

Berger summarized the history of native governments and the affirmation of communal land tenure, and then recommended that natives be allowed their distinctive institutions of self-government and modes of land tenure. Native lands should be retribalized by transferring them to tribal governments. This form of landholding "reflects their own cultural imperatives and ensures that ancestral lands will remain in their possession, under their own governance."

In addition to recommending that corporate lands be transferred to tribal governments, Berger also advocated that "the members of Alaska Native tribes should have exclusive hunting and fishing rights and jurisdiction over Native lands and waters, and shared rights and jurisdiction over state and federal lands and waters." Finally, tribal governments established in all of Alaska's native villages should assert their native sovereignty, and "the state should recognize tribal governments as appropriate local governments for all purposes under state law."

Justice Berger continued, "[T]he clock cannot be turned back, nor can the rule of discovery be vitiated on any retroactive basis: the reality of effective occupation stands in the way." Nevertheless, native peoples should be accorded some measure of self-rule within the constitutional framework of any Western nation. Indigenous groups "are making many proposals" encompassing "renewable and non-renewable resources, education, health, social services, and public order and they extend to the shape and structure of political institutions." In conclusion, Berger declared that "these should be opportunities to affirm our commitment to the human rights" of native peoples. In the meantime, Alaska's natives considered changes to ANCSA.

In March of 1985, the special convention of the Alaska Federation of Natives approved eight resolutions setting the framework for legislative changes to be sought in the Alaska Native Claims Settlement Act of 1971. The desired changes proposed solutions to the critical problems of land protection, stock retention, and the inclusion of all natives in the benefits of the Settlements Act. Shortly thereafter, Monroe E. Price, the dean of the Benjamin N. Cardozo School of Law, Yeshiva University, in New York City, transmitted proposed draft legislation embodying the recently adopted resolutions seeking changes in the ANCSA.

In December 1987, the U.S. House and Senate passed the amendments to the ANCSA and President Ronald Reagan signed the measure into law on 3 February 1988. It clarified the ANCSA and took care of some of the concerns natives had expressed about stock and land ownership after

1991, as well as numerous other problems.

The year is 2001, thirty years after President Nixon signed the Alaska Native Claims Settlement Act into law. Proponents and opponents have called the ANCSA either the most generous settlement Congress has ever passed for any group of natives, or the death knell for Alaska's native cultures. Without doubt, the last thirty years have witnessed confusion, turmoil, great financial losses, and bitter debates among the beneficiaries of ANCSA about what the future should look like. What is certain is that the majority culture must attempt to finds ways of preserving the remnants of the aboriginal hunting and gathering societies. Our increasingly uniform world society would be the poorer for losing them.

It is clear today that the thirteen Alaska Native Regional Corporations (the thirteenth was added later for Alaska natives who had moved out of state, to whom Congress denied a land base but granted cash) are wealthier and own more private land in the forty-ninth state than any other economic sector. The subsidiaries, about 200 of them, span the state and circle the globe. These regional corporations are involved in many enterprises, including services, construction, timber, security, real estate, government contracting, tourism, and telecommunications. Despite difficult starts, all are earning profits, and many have flourished.

The Arctic Slope Regional Corporation, representing 7,933 shareholders, posted 1999 revenues of $888 million, up from $663 million the previous year, an increase of 25.32 percent. It had 5,162 employees, and the Alaska Business Monthly of September 2000 listed it as the number-one corporation in its summary of "Top 49ers," the forty-nine biggest businesses in Alaska. Established in 1972, its key personnel are Oliver Leavitt, chairman, Jacob Adams, president, and Conrad Bagne,

CAO-Corp. Counsel. Like the 12 other corporations, Arctic Slope Regional Corporation grew slowly at first and has suffered numerous setbacks over the years. However, it posted revenues of $466.2 million in 1994, $468.5 million in 1995, $530.0 million the next year, and in 1997 $662.8 million. ASRC is a diversified holding company with over forty subsidiaries. Among these are SKW/Eskimos, Inc., engaged in general construction; Puget Plastics Corp., plastics manufacturing; Natchiq Inc., oilfield services and fabrication; Eskimos Inc., fuel and product distribution; ASCG Incorporated, engineering; ASRC Aerospace, aerospace engineering; ASRC Tundra Tours Inc., Top of the World Hotel in Barrow; Arctic Slope World Services Inc., government services and airline support; Alaska Growth Capital, BIDCO, financial services; and Arctic Slope Construction Inc., design/build and environmental service.

Obviously, the changes in the last three decades have been swift. Modernization has had an impact on traditional Eskimo culture and the Inupiaq language has declined dramatically. About 15,000 Eskimos live in the language area from Unalakleet to Barter Island. Of these, only about 3,500 are fluent in the language, and many are elderly. Many fear that when they die their culture will die with them. To counter this rapid decline, several immersion programs are underway in the Inupiaq language area. In addition, the Eskimos have established and operate Illisagvik College in Barrow.

North Slope communities have seen much investment in basic infrastructure, such as sewer and water, roads, housing, reliable electric services, and various other modern conveniences of life.

In short, when President Richard M. Nixon signed the Alaska Native Claims Settlement Act in 1971 he set in motion vast changes in the forth-

ninth state. John Hope, a Tlingit and a Juneau resident involved in the land claims struggle, described the years that followed the ANCSA settlement: "It's like you and I never saw a baseball game in our lives. We'd never seen mitts or bats or baseballs. All of a sudden you were told here are your mitts. Here are your bats. Here are your balls. Tomorrow, you play the Yankees."

Despite many problems, some of the Native Regional Corporations have grown to become all-star players, not only in Alaska but also in the contiguous states. Arctic Slope Regional Corporation on the top of the continent is the largest Alaskan-owned company. In addition to its many activities, it plans to expand into fiber optic installations and specialty engineering in the near future. Chairman Leavitt remarked that "our goal is to be a billion dollar company by 2001. Our directors made that a vision and a dream, and we'll probably attain it."

It is clear that the Eskimos have survived and adapted to the radical changes that have occurred since ANCSA. Their culture will survive, albeit vastly modified. With educational opportunities beckoning, many young people leave the villages and do not return. Subsistence still plays a part, but the resource base cannot sustain the population, which is so much greater than in previous centuries. Most regrettably, the languages are being lost, although both the regional and the village corporations have programs to keep them alive.

A group of Inuit and white children hamming it up during ITC Annual General Meeting, Nain Labrador, May 1994.

PHOTOGRAPH BY HANS-LUDWIG BLOHM.